CYBERSPACE
FOR KIDS

GRADES 1-2
600 SITES THAT ARE KID-TESTED AND PARENT-APPROVED

By the Mandel Family

Cover Illustration by
Peggy Jackson

Inside Illustrations by
Marty Bucella

Publisher
Instructional Fair · TS Denison
Grand Rapids, Michigan 49544

▲▼▲

Instructional Fair · TS Denison

Credits
Authors: the Mandel family
Cover Artist: Peggy Jackson
Inside Illustration: Marty Bucella
Project Director/Editor: Danielle de Gregory
Art Production: Darcy Bell-Myers
Graphic Layout: Laurie Ford

About the Authors
The Mandel family consists of Mom, Dad, and their six kids. In the process of home schooling her four oldest kids, Mimi Mandel sent her young students on a world tour—via the Internet. The *Cyberspace for Kids* series is a result of those travels—a homework project that developed into four books and a publishing contract as well as a wealth of knowledge and experiences along the journey.

Standard Book Number:1-56822-873-2
Cyberspace for Kids Grades 1–2
Copyright © 1999 by Ideal • Instructional Fair Publishing Group
a division of Tribune Education
2400 Turner Avenue NW
Grand Rapids, Michigan 49544

All Rights Reserved • Printed in the USA

Table of Contents

Welcome to Cyberspace

C'mon in. Take your shoes off and leave everything you think you already know at the door. You're about to embark on a wonderful journey through a world without boundaries. It's a world where anything can happen and anyone can appear. It's a world that you, along with millions of other people around the globe, will call home. With some help from us, of course.

This guide is chock full of resources that will help you to:

- Find out just what the Internet, World Wide Web, and Cyberspace are. (Hint: they're pretty much the same thing.)
- Communicate with friends and relatives anywhere in the world (yes, unfortunately, even Uncle Bernie).
- Find friends who are interested in the same things you like.
- Learn everything from astronomy to zoology from thousands of information databases and libraries (where you can talk as loud as you want).
- Download games, books, information, articles, and even computer programs for free.
- Hear news and sports practically as it happens.
- Play the latest games against the computer or people hundreds of miles away.
- Shop in a range of unique stores to buy everything from paintball guns to baseball cards.
- Research every subject you could possibly dream of — including dreams.
- Build your very own web site (where you finally get to make the rules).
- Visit zoos and museums around the globe.
- Take a virtual trip to every imaginable spot on earth (including that biggest ball of twine).
- Take classes from on-line schools, universities, or organizations.
- Chat with people from next door or across the continents.
- Access organizations or find that special shoelace collecting group.
- Read full-length books (or even short ones).
- Listen to historical speeches or your favorite tunes.
- Watch live video and animation.
- Have more fun than you could possibly imagine.

Traveling through cyberspace is an exciting adventure with no speed limits. But, like those family trips, you're going to need to bring a few things along for the journey: a willingness to learn and an adventurous spirit; a sprinkle of wisdom to know where to click and when to skip; an ability to evaluate what is a time stealer and what is a time stopper; and, snacks, plenty of snacks—hey, it's a great big virtual world out there and virtual food is about as appetizing as last night's liver (blech).

Keep in mind, though, that traveling the Internet is like wandering through a foreign country. You're going to encounter a new language and become overwhelmed with all of the new things to see and do. But soon, you'll be a veteran traveler and be able to enjoy all the sights and sounds of this new frontier. And don't be surprised if you get lost. (Sometimes, that's half the fun.) So, remember, don't get discouraged.

We've carefully selected the best of the best web sites for kids just like us. And believe us, if it kept this tough group interested long enough to write down the web site, then it's definitely worth checking out. But before you start with all of these best places to see in cyberspace, take a walk through our chapters to find out what the Internet is, how it got started, and the many ways you can use it. And, as always, remember to have fun.

The Internet and the World Wide Web

What Is the Internet?

The word Internet means network of networks. It is thousands of smaller networks connected by cables scattered all over the globe. Think of it as gum in your hair, with the networks being each strand of hair and the gum is the cables holding it all together. On any given day, it connects roughly 15 million users in over 50 countries.

The most popular and well-known part of the Internet is the World Wide Web. The World Wide Web is where home pages brimming with graphics, sound, and text are located. The Internet is much larger. It includes gopher, telnet, usenet, bitnet, and a whole bunch of "nets" that aren't too colorful or exciting. They are mostly gigantic lists of information that go on and on. You could stay busy on just the WWW part of the Internet for about the next 1,000 years, so we won't be going into the other "nets" after this short intro.

How Was the Internet Created?

The Internet began way back in the 1960s. It all started when a scientist figured there should be a way to share research and ideas. One problem. How do you do that when you are stretched out over five different continents? The Internet saved the day! Now those people trying to find a cure for cancer can communicate instantly!

In the 1990s, the Internet continues to grow at lightening speed. Some estimate that the number of messages transferred increases by 20 percent a month. In the beginning, the backbone of the Internet moved data at 56,000 bits per second. That proved too slow to move the increasing amounts of data. In the last few years, the maximum speed was increased to 1.5 million and then 45 million bits per second. Internet experts are always hard at work trying to figure out how to make the system faster and faster. Now they are trying to figure out how to pump data at speeds of up to 2 billion bits per second—fast enough to send a huge encyclopedia across the United States in seconds.

Another major change has been the development of commercial services. Companies have come to realize the power of the Internet. They are using the Internet to attract the people to whom they want to sell products and services. What began as a small government experiment is now an enormous private enterprise. Have you noticed that on almost every television commercial they now list a web site address? Didn't see that when you were a little kid, huh?

What Is the Information Superhighway?

Has anyone ever called you by a nickname? The Internet has been nicknamed the "Information Superhighway." That's because it is kind of like an enormous map of highways. Instead of cars, computers transport information. Imagine an intricate network of transcontinental superhighways connecting huge metropolitan cities. Out of these large cities come smaller highways that link to smaller cities. Within those small cities are single lane roads. Out of those roads are small streets where residents live. The Internet is just like this road system except that it is a mass of cables and computers instead of highways and roads.

How Fast Does the Internet Go?

The Internet can move information at speeds that are so fast it is impossible to compare them to anything we've known in the past. Even faster than your mom can say "Go to your room." (Now, that's fast!) The backbone of the Internet sends data at rates of 45 million bits per second. The modem in your home moves about 28,800 to 56,000 bits per second. Connected to the backbone computers are smaller networks that send the information to smaller geographic areas. These move data at speeds of around 1.5 million bits per second. Feeding off of the smaller networks are even tinier networks. These smaller networks feed into your own personal computer. Just think of it like a humongous funnel with all the information circling down to the tiny hole where your computer sits.

Some people assume there must be one Godzilla-like sized computer running the Internet. Actually, it is made up of literally millions of separate computers. The Internet has no center, no top, and no bottom. There is no master editor or Grand Poohbah of Cyberspace. No one can decide if you come or go. Anyone can put up a page or take it down. You do not need permission to create a web page. This freedom can be used for good or bad. One good thing is that the Internet can never break down. If one computer fails, the rest of the network can still operate. And, believe us, one computer can and will crash. Ours does more than we care to remember.

The major problem is that with so many thousands of computers connected, it can be difficult to find exactly what you want. There are often traffic jams when too many people want to go to the same location, causing people to have to wait and wait and wait to get in to the site. It's kinda like trying to get into the bathroom when your brother or sister is hogging it.

The way the Internet works is complicated, but it really boils down to communication. Your words can race around the world in seconds. You can visit small informal home pages of individual people or other kids. You can go to megasites where major companies have 4 million products for sale. You can hear music, see videos, and watch cartoons on-line. You can chat with someone in the Arctic and write to a pen pal from Australia. You'll read poems, short stories, and recipes. Things will touch you, make you mad, cry, and laugh. You'll be exposed to new ideas and some you wish you'd never heard of. You'll encounter different types of people and some you'd rather not have known. You'll do this all within a community that transcends geographic borders, language barriers, and ethnic differences. Just one great big melting pot.

How Do I Surf the Net?

When you open a book, you usually start at the beginning. But the problem with the Internet is, there's no beginning, or even any end to it. You can look at it from many points of view. You can weave in and out. You can jump from one idea to another in a millisecond. Let's take a closer look at how the Internet is designed, which should help explain how to move around it.

The Internet is a bunch of different services. They are Gopher, Archie, Veronica, Telnet, Bitnet, Usenet, Relay Chat, and, what we think is the best part of the Internet, the World Wide Web. The World Wide Web is the part of the Internet filled with pictures, graphics, animations, video, and audio. It's composed of pages that you can get to by punching in an address, which is called an URL.

What Is a URL?

URL stands for Universal Resource Locator. It is a key to getting where you want to go on the Internet. This is what a typical URL looks like:

http://www.themandelkids.com

http://www. means "HyperText Transport Protocol://World Wide Web. It is a shorthand term to describe the way the Web moves information throughout the networks and around the world.

These can be:

www	located on the World Wide Web
gopher	located on a Gopher server
news	located on a Usenet news group
ftp	located on an FTP server.

Next, comes the name of the site you want to visit, such as "themandelkids." This tells the Internet the exact page you want. And, finally, comes the domain name, which gives you a clue as to what type of organization it is:

edu	U.S. educational institution
com	commercial organization
org	non-profit organization
gov	government organization

And these are just the beginning. New domain names are being added to accommodate the growing number of web sites, much like new area codes are constantly being created to handle all of the new telephone numbers.

URL Problems

If at first you don't succeed in getting to a site, try, try, again. The most common reason for a URL to fail is a typo. Look closely and see if anything is misspelled. A URL can't contain blank spaces. When you type a URL into your browser, make sure that you correctly type the letters that are supposed to be capitalized and the letters that are supposed to be lowercase. URLs are case sensitive, so the smallest deviation from the correct letters can make it impossible for you to get to the right location. The URL should end either with a domain name or with a file name.

What Does "404, File Not Found" Mean?

It's pretty common to receive an error message "404, File Not Found." This means the web server could not find a file matching that URL. Try again later or check to make sure you typed the URL correctly. In addition, it may mean that this URL doesn't even exist anymore and is now just a fond memory of electrons.

Second Commandment: Abide by the moral and legal standards of society.

In the cyberworld, you are known only by your e-mail address and your words. Some kids interpret this as the freedom to lie or be mean. Don't.

Breaking the law is, of course, totally bad netiquette. It is illegal to use the Internet to do something illegal. It is wrong to use the computer to steal property, information, or people's time. Another example of being ethical is, if you use shareware, you should pay for it. Paying for shareware encourages more people to write shareware. And, it is only fair to compensate the person who created the software, if it is something that you use.

Third Commandment: Lurk before you leap.

When you enter a chat room or newsgroup, spend some time reading the messages and listening to the chat to get a feel for what is going on. This is called "lurking." After you are familiar with how the people in there act, go ahead and join in.

Fourth Commandment: Respect other people's time and bandwidth.

When you send e-mail to a discussion group, you're asking many other people to read your message. This takes time. It's your responsibility to ensure that the time they spend reading your posting (message) isn't wasted.

This brings up the issue of how many copies to send. It is so easy to copy to people when using e-mail that many copies are sent unnecessarily. They waste time and bandwidth. Before you send a copy, ask yourself whether that person really needs to know the information. (Especially if it has to do with your squashed bug collection. No one really wants to know about that . . .)

Fifth Commandment: Remember who your audience is.

The whole world, including you! It is best to assume that everyone in the world may read your words. Though e-mail is sent to only one person, it is very easy to forward an e-mail message to hundreds or thousands of people (including your punish-happy parents, so be careful).

Sixth Commandment: Use your time wisely by making smart choices.

In order to get anywhere on the Web, you must choose where you wish to go. If you don't know where you are going, how do you know how to get there? With such a vast mountain of information available on-line—way more than one person could ever read, you need to be very careful not to waste your time.

Seventh Commandment: Strive to do your best in form and substance.

As was mentioned earlier, you never know who will be reading what you write. The principal of your school or perhaps the President of the United States may decide to listen in on a newsgroup to which you post. Or, imagine, for just a minute, that someone forwarded one of your e-mail messages to your teacher.

We would all like to think that we make a good impression. In the virtual world, your writing is the only way you have to make a good impression. If you write well, you will likely come off as educated, intelligent, and respectable. If you compose hastily and sloppily, however, your audience may perceive you, perhaps inaccurately, as uneducated and unintelligent. If you want to make a good impression on those out in the cyberworld, it's a good idea to make your writing look great.

Eighth Commandment: **Forgive as you would want to be forgiven.**

Sometimes it's tempting to tear someone apart for an obvious grammatical error, misspelling, or blatant display of stupidity. What we must keep in mind, though, is that what we are reading is only one small piece of the person on the other end, who is typing away just like we are. Perhaps he or she was uninformed—or in a hurry—or simply made a mistake. Give that person a break, just like you would want one.

Ninth Commandment: **Be helpful to newbies.**

We were all new at one time or another and needed a helping hand. And although you may have a better head start with this book, others may not. So if you meet someone who is new to the Internet, stop for a minute and show her or him around the place. You will be glad you did.

Tenth Commandment: **Don't use foul language.**

This will get you kicked off faster than you can say "No @&#% swearing in cyberspace."

And most important, that old hidden *Eleventh Commandment:* **Have an adult help you when you "surf" the Internet.**

The Internet is a great place with lots of things to do. But there are also places from which you should stay away. An adult can help you to explore the good and stay away from the bad. You can see what a "good" site is when you visit us at: http://www.themandelkids.com.

E-mail in Cyberspace

What Is E-mail?

E-mail simply stands for electronic mail. It's sort of a cross between the post office and the telephone, only e-mail is as fast as, but much cheaper than, a phone call. Plus it is faster than postal mail.

With postal mail, you have to write it, put it in an envelope, get a stamp, put it in a mailbox, and send it across many miles over sea or land. Maybe you'll get lucky and it'll arrive a week later. Whew. Then there is e-mail! All you have to do with e-mail is write it on the computer and, with a click of your finger, send it on its way. Presto! It usually arrives within seconds. And did we mention that, if you have access to the Internet, it's free? You don't have to worry about stamps, or being sent to your room for running up your parents' phone bill.

Another great thing about e-mail is that the Internet never closes like a post office. You can read and respond to mail 24 hours a day.

What Does E-mail Do?

E-mail lets you communicate to other people all over the world. You can find pen pals in the farthest corners of the globe like South Africa or Antarctica; send a quick message to your best friend who lives across the street; or remind Aunt Gertrude that you have plenty of Christmas sweaters already. If someone has access to a computer and the Internet, you can send that person an e-mail. All you need is an e-mail address.

What's an E-mail Address?

Just like your house address is where your home is located, an e-mail address is where you're located on the Internet. It's the key to getting and sending messages across the Internet. It is placed on your message itself (this tells the message where to go) and follows this format: yourname@nameof-provider.com. For instance, in contacting one of the Mandel kids, Jeremy, you'd write: jeremy@the-mandelkids.com. You don't even need your own personal computer, you can use one at your school or at the library. All you need is access to the Internet where you can set up an account for free.

When Did E-mail Begin?

E-mail wasn't always the e-mail that you know today. Did you know that e-mail started back in 1972 just so a group of about 100 scientists could talk to each other? Today, there's more than 60 million people zipping e-mails back and forth, making it the most widely used tool on the Internet. By the year 2001, half of the population in the United States will communicate via e-mail. That's 135 million people who will send more than 500 million messages a day. And by the year 2005, people will be sending more than 5 billion personal messages a day. There are a lot of postal carriers that are glad they won't have to deliver all of that! Kinda makes you wonder if people will still talk face-to-face by then, doesn't it?

How Long Should an E-mail Be?

Unlike that mandatory history paper, e-mails can be whatever length you want, as long as a book, or as short as a word. And, you can even attach something to it. (It's okay, it won't fall off in transit.) Just click the "Attach" button on your e-mail software and it will ask you what you want to attach. It can be a file that has your latest homework assignment in it, a favorite web site address, or that picture of your dad in his pink striped Bermuda shorts (shudder).

Can I Send the Same E-mail to More Than One Person?

Sure (well, as long as you know more than one person, of course). E-mail can be sent to as many people as you can fit in the Address list of the e-mail (which is more than you can count.). You can send it to those people by either listing them in the Addressee section, or in the CC, which means Carbon Copy, section. And for those of you who don't remember the time before you were born, you probably don't know what "carbon" means. Before photocopy machines, you needed carbon paper and a blank sheet of paper to put between your typing or writing to make a copy. That's where CC gets its name.

Why Should I Use E-mail?

The same reason you should eat spinach—it's good for you. Actually, it's one of the fastest, cheapest ways to talk to someone, but with it, comes responsibility. There's a new language you must learn and a new set of rules and responsibilities you should know.

What Are Some Rules to Help Me Send Better E-mails?

Be concise.

One of the best things about e-mail is how quickly and informally you can say something. Keeping your thoughts short is especially important when posting a message to a newsgroup or a mailing list. Often, people review hundreds of messages at a time. They are probably not so keen to hear about your dog's escape into the neighbor's rose garden. A good poster is one who gets right to the point.

Avoid flames.

No, you don't have to stop, drop, and roll. An e-mail flame is a mean or nasty message that is sent to you. And no one likes them. So, as the golden rule decrees, don't do it and it won't be done unto you. And remember that whatever you type has a way of being sent around from person to person. Your neighbors, teachers, friends,and parents, as well as strangers, could be reading what you type. Mom was right on this one—if you don't have something nice to say, don't say anything at all.

Don't repeat the same message.

Sending the same e-mail twice to someone is as annoying as your little brother on Saturday mornings. It is best to give people a chance to respond to a previous message before re-sending the original message. Many people send and receive e-mail only once a day or just once a week. Give people time to read your message since not everyone checks their e-mail every five minutes.

Don't overuse mailing lists.

When you're sending a message to many people, a huge list of other e-mail addresses appears at the beginning of the message. This can make your message seem like junk mail.

Be yourself

Somebody famous once said "To thine own self be true." Which boils down to this: Be yourself; don't pretend to be somebody else. That has never been more important than on-line where it may be tempting to become someone else since no one is looking.

How Do I Sign My E-mails?

Not signing your e-mail is like not eating the cherry on top of the ice cream. It leaves an empty craving inside. In addition, this can be yet another way to express yourself. Whether it's formal or funny, quick or quirky, e-mail allows you to end with your own personal style. Most e-mail software allows you to choose a set signature that can include a quote or saying or emoticon or nickname. Every time you "sign off," you just click on the "Signature" button and it will appear. Or, you can always just type it in manually so that your final words suit the tone and purpose of that specific letter.

Want To Try Your First E-mail?

We would love to hear from you . . . so e-mail us already. Sometimes it takes a little while for us to write back, since Dad keeps hogging the computer to play "Tetris," but we promise that we will. Here are our addresses:

Aliza@themandelkids.com

Jeremy@themandelkids.com

Wendy@themandelkids.com

Corey@themandelkids.com

MomMandel@themandelkids.com

DadMandel@themandelkids.com

Newsgroups in Cyberspace

What Is a Newsgroup?

Do you have friends who get together and talk about baseball? Dance class? Or even video games? Well, put them on the Internet and you'll have a newsgroup (not to mention some really high-voltage friends). A newsgroup is simply a discussion on the Internet about a specific topic of your choice. However, it is not conducted through talking, but instead, through posting messages—just as though you were using a bulletin board or an answering machine. These discussions can last just a few hours or stretch out over days. Just pick a subject, any subject, and you can bet there is a newsgroup out there for it.

Who Uses Them?

Millions of people use newsgroups, including you. Every day, over 100 million characters are typed into the system. This is the equivalent of nearly an encyclopedia's (the kind with one volume for each letter of the alphabet) worth of words. With that immense flow of messages, everyone can find a group that is interesting to them.

What Is Usenet?

Usenet is like the Internet, only instead of a collection of networks, it's a collection of newsgroups. The Usenet covers every imaginable topic from astronomy to magic tricks to zoos. *CAUTION:* The language and content of some newsgroups can be R-rated or even worse. Remember, sticks and stones can break your bones, but words can permanently scar you!

How Do I Find a Newsgroup?

The very first place you should check out is: news.announce.newusers which is for brand new users like you. Here, you'll find some articles that will help you to understand more about the Internet and newsgroups in general.

Once you're ready to move on to other newsgroups, you first have to realize that it's a great big newsgroup world out there. Almost too big. That's why the listing of available newsgroups has been divided into several big categories. Choose one of those and you'll then be given a list of newsgroups in that category. Got one that looks good? Well, then, click on it and, you guessed it, you'll be given another list of sub-categories within that broad topic. It may take a minute or two to find the newsgroup you're looking for, but in the end it's all worth it.

The newsgroup names all start with a main category heading that will help you find your specific area of interest. For example, those that have "rec" at the beginning are related to hobbies, games, and recreational themes. Here are some examples of kid's newsgroups:

alt.kids-talk: Discussion group for kids
alt.tv.simpsons: *The Simpsons*
k12.chat.elementary: Discussions for students in grades K–5
rec.arts.comics.marketplace: Comic book classified ads
rec.arts.disney: Discussions about Disney

rec.collecting.cards: For cards and collectibles collectors
rec.equestrian: Discussions about horses
rec.games.misc: Games
rec.music.video: Discussions about music videos

And that's just the tip of the newsgroup iceberg. And we're talking an iceberg that could sink several *Titanics.* More categories are being added as Usenet grows and grows—kinda like that green stuff on the cheese in the back of our refrigerator (let's not ever talk of that again).

With such a massive list to select from, you will probably want to have your own customized Usenet list. You can search for groups that you like, read them for awhile to see if they are interesting, and then save them as bookmarks in your computer so they will be easier to access.

How Does a Newsgroup Work?

You may be wondering exactly how one of these newsgroups works. It's as simple as talking, really. One person writes a message and posts it in the newsgroup. Then, somebody else responds to the message. Soon, a thread of conversation begins.

What Is a Thread?

No, it's not that stuff you sew patches on your jeans with. A "thread" refers to a strand of conversation about one topic within that category. For example, if the group is for teenagers who are home-schooling, the thread might be about volunteer opportunities that those kids have explored. Following these threads is relatively easy. Usually these messages are grouped together. When you read one message, you can hit "Next" to read the next related message. As you explore Usenet, we recommend that you read some of the messages first before you jump in. This is called "lurking."

What Is Lurking?

Lurking is like standing by the punch bowl at a dance and watching everyone else have fun. In the beginning, it's not a bad idea. It's smart to listen in for a while just to get a feel for that particular newsgroup. You'll soon find out that each newsgroup has its own personality. Once you spend some time "lurking," you will see what the common themes are and what flavor the conversation takes. Then you can jump right in.

How Do I Join?

When you are ready to say something, you can introduce yourself as a newcomer to the group, or just join right in an ongoing conversation, or you can start a whole new thread. It is encouraged to ask questions, but first you may want to ask if there is a FAQ list, which is a list of Frequently Asked Questions, so you don't bug people with the same question that's been asked by every newcomer that came along.

When you add something to a discussion, you may choose to copy the posting you are responding to within your message. This is a good idea so that people can see what you're responding to, just in case the original message has disappeared from their systems.

▲▼▲

What Is Cross-Posting?

At times, you may have an idea that should be heard in more than one group. This process is called cross-posting. Instead of posting individual messages to several different groups, you can post the same message to many groups at the same time. Easy on you, easy on them.

Cross-posting is simple. All you have to do is type the names of the various groups, separated by a comma, but no space, and hit "Enter."

And, while cross-posting can help to communicate your thoughts to numerous groups that overlap in nature, you don't want to post to an excessive number of them or to the wrong newsgroup. If you do, you will most likely be flamed.

What Is a Flame?

A flame is a nasty attack on somebody for what they have written. No, they don't find your house and wait for you in the bushes; they do it over postings. Periodically, an exchange of flames erupts into a flame war that begins to take up all the space in a given newsgroup. These can go on for weeks, months, and some say, even years. Often, just when they're dying down, somebody new to the flame war reads all the messages, gets upset, and starts it all over again. But, when the newsgroup suddenly becomes just flames, an urgent plea is made that the flame war be taken to e-mail so everybody else can get back to whatever the newsgroup's topic is.

Whom Might I Find on Newsgroups?

Net.weenies: These are the kind of people who post nasty messages just because they have nothing better to do. Or, they're tasty little hot dogs—we can't figure out which.

Net.geeks: These are people for whom the Internet is their life. (Careful, you may become such an animal).

Lurkers: Invisible, but still there behind computer screens reading every message, they read everything in a newsgroup but never post or respond.

Wizards: These are people who are experts on a specific topic and actively share their knowledge (and maybe a few tricks).

Net.saints: Saints are those who are willing to answer newcomers' questions. They eagerly share their knowledge and offer their expertise or words of wisdom.

Chatting in Cyberspace

What is Chatting?

Chatting is communication that happens in real time. Ever talk to your best friend? That's chatting. Congratulations, you've been an official chatter all of your life. But now, you get to learn how to do it in cyberspace. But don't worry, it's easy. Just like talking to your friend, chatting occurs right away. The difference is that it's done by moving the buttons on the keyboard instead of moving your mouth.

What Is a Chat Room?

A chat room is a place in cyberspace where you can talk to other people. There can be two people or hundreds. The conversation can be serious, clever, boring, or meaningless (kinda like reading your sister's diary). You can make friends or enemies and you'll never know just who might join in. You may talk to one person, while others talk around you, or to the whole chat room at once.

Chat rooms are usually organized around various subjects and are geared towards adults or kids and teens. But remember, because people can't be seen through the computer, you can never be sure exactly to whom you're talking. So, it's super important that you never give out personal information in a chat room.

Chat rooms can be confusing and intimidating when you first enter. On the screen, people's sentences appear like a play with one person speaking after the other. But because you can't actually hear them, sometimes conversations can get confusing if they're not grouped together. What happens is that someone asks a question while at the same time, another person is answering something entirely different. You just have to read what's going on and follow it for a few seconds. You'll soon see just who is talking to whom. When you get experienced enough, you'll soon have several conversations going at the same time. All you have to do is just jump in and chat away—you'll be a chatterbox in no time.

What If I Misunderstand?

Sometimes it is hard to understand just what a person is saying to you in a chat room because you can't hear the tone of voice. This happens a lot in chat rooms. Words that appear on a computer can seem impersonal and cold; they don't always communicate exactly what we mean. You can't see the person's facial expressions or other types of body language that are cues to what the person really means. Here's an example of how three words can mean very different things depending on how they're said.

"Thanks a lot."

Which does this mean?

"Thank you very much, I appreciate what you did," OR
"Thanks, but no thanks."

In person, you'd have no problem figuring out which sentence the person meant. But when chatting, it's sometimes difficult to determine how it was meant because you can't see or hear the person. When in doubt, it's best to ask.

What Is an Emoticon?

This robotic-sounding name is anything but. Combining the words emotion and icon, emoticons are the way chatters attach tone of voice and body language to their words. This helps solve the misunderstanding of sentences. Chatters can give hugs, grin, offer snacks or drinks, wink, or even hit heads with a foam mallet. A good example is a winking smilie face, shown as ;). Emoticons open up a whole new world of talking. And when you receive one, it's best to play along.

Is There Any Other Way Chatters Express Themselves?

Experienced chatters sprinkle their messages with abbreviations. This is typing a word with just a few letters. "Before" becomes "b4." Abbreviations save eons of time typing when you're at the helm of a conversation that's moving at the speed of light. On-line, most abbreviations are acronyms. What are acronyms? These are three or four letters that stand for a phrase, like "FAQ" which means "Frequently Asked Questions." To impress your friends, just sprinkle your next e-mail liberally with acronyms.

If you keep the basic rules of on-line netiquette and safety tucked in your back pocket, chatting can be a fun way to meet new people, hear other points of view, and just waste some good old-fashioned "study" time.

Note to Parents and Teachers

There are many valuable educational insights that students as young the first and second graders may gain while becoming acquainted with the Internet. There are, however, not a great many sites which are geared only towards this age group. Some of the sites that have been included in this book have a reading level beyond that of the primary grades. These sites are well worth visiting because of their superior visual content. Please spend time guiding your first and second graders around the Web so that they may take full advantage of the sites listed in this book.

Safety in Cyberspace

Why Worry About Safety?

The number of things to do on-line is constantly growing. You can check the news, weather, sports, stock quotes, and movie reviews. You can shop, trade stocks, do banking, and pay bills on-line. As we have seen, millions of people communicate through e-mail. You can meet people in public message boards, in chat rooms, and in newsgroups.

Whenever you are interacting with other people, there are some inherent dangers. Most people have mainly positive experiences on-line. Like anything you do, whether it be driving in a car or swimming in the pool, there are risks. The on-line world, like the rest of society, is made up of human beings. Most are honest and well-intentioned, but some may be rude, obnoxious, or insulting. Some may even be downright mean and dangerous. The on-line world mirrors the real one; it includes the good, the bad, and the ugly.

While you can have a ton of fun on-line, you can also be the target of crime and exploitation. More than ever, you need an adult's help to stay safe. Please feel free to photocopy My Rules for On-line Safety and post them near your computer. Following these rules will help make your experiences in cyberspace happy, healthy, and productive.

What Are the Dangers?

Whenever you use the computer unsupervised, you run the following risks.

Exposure to Inappropriate Material

You may see inappropriate pictures or words of a sexual or violent nature.

Physical Danger

You might provide information or arrange an encounter that could pose a threat to your safety.

Harassment

You might be sent e-mail or bulletin board messages that are harassing, demeaning, or belligerent.

My Rules for On-line Safety

1. I will not give out any personal information such as my address, telephone number, or parents' places of work.

2. I will not give out the addresses, telephone numbers, or the names of my school or after-school activities.

3. I will tell my parents immediately if I see anything or anyone that makes me feel uncomfortable.

4. I will never agree to get together with someone I met on-line without first checking with my parents.

5. I will never send a person my picture or anything else personal without first checking with my parents.

6. I will not respond to any messages that are mean or that in any way make me feel uncomfortable. It is not my fault if I get a message like that. If I do, I will tell my parents right away so that they can report it to the on-line service.

7. I will talk with my parents so that we can set up rules for going on-line. We will decide upon the time of day that I can be on-line, the length of time I can be on-line, and appropriate areas for me to visit.

8. I will not access other areas or break these rules without my parents' permission.

▲▼

AES Bug Club Home Page

http://www.ex.ac.uk/bugclub/welcome.html

Do you want to Cuddle a Cockroach, Stroke a Stick Insect, or Hug a Harvestman? Then this Bug Club site is just for you. This site has information that will "insect" you with bug fever.

The Adventures of Alex

http://www.alextheape.com/

Travel north of nowhere and west of wherever to Comfort Cove, home of Alex the Ape, the khaki-clad environmental hero. Together with his Creature Comforts Crew, Alex protects his Mystic Jungle homeland from any and all evil forces. C'mon along as these jungle jammers enter their next wild adventures.

Animal Connection

http://www.cyberark.com/

Ever wanted to talk to the animals? Discover the fascinating world of interspecies telepathic communication and find out how to naturally cure your pet's ailments. For the true animal lover.

At The Farm

http://miksike.com/unit/

Old McDonald's farm was nothing like this! Take an interactive journey with Margarita as she discovers everything there is to know about living on a farm—from pig farming to crop cultivation. You'll be wearing suspenders and a straw hat in no time.

B-EYE: The world through the eyes of a bee
http://cvs.anu.edu.au/andy/beye/beyehome.html

Have you ever wondered how other creatures view the world? Now you can see the world through the eyes of a honeybee. Why? Just BEE-cause.

The Bear Den
http://www.nature-net.com/bears/

Since not all bears are like Yogi and Boo Boo, this site offers some information on just what wilderness bears are really like. Pictures are plentiful as you learn about eight different species of bears.

Best of Breed Online
http://w3.mgr.com/mgr/howell/bobpages/mainmenu.htm

Your faithful friend's friend on the Internet. Probably the world's most authoritative, comprehensive, and useful resource on dogs, it offers pictures and information on any breed of dog there is.

Big Cats On-line
http://dialspace.dial.pipex.com/agarman/

A purrrrfectly giant site that cat-alogs every BIG cat species, including lions, leopards, tigers, jaguars, and more. View pictures and information on how these wild cats live and why they might be in danger.

▲▼

The Bigger Cats Information Page

http://www.lam.mus.ca.us/~pcannon/cats.html

Jaguars, cougars, and pumas. At this site you'll discover dozens of interesting pages about those BIG cats otherwise known as lions and tigers. Oh my.

Birch Aquarium at Scripps Introduction Page

http://aqua.ucsd.edu/

An ocean of knowledge—the Birch Aquarium explains how an ocean environment sustains itself, why the oceans are so important, and any other fishy information you want to know.

Brevard Zoo

http://www.brevardzoo.org/

Go on a virtual tour and see the lemurs and the gibbons. Check out the big collection of animal photographs as well.

Bugs in the News!

http://falcon.cc.ukans.edu/~jbrown/bugs.html

This web site is all about microbiology. Microbiology is the study of things that are really, really teeny. These things are so small that they can only be seen under a powerful microscope. You can learn about viruses and bacteria and antibiotics.

The Butterfly Web Site
http://www.butterflyweb site.com

Flitter among the flowers with the beautiful butterflies—caught for you on this page. Did you know there are many types of butterflies? Find out just how many and why they do the things that they do.

Carnegie Museum of Natural History
http://www.clpgh.org/cmnh/

This is one of the six largest natural history museums in the United States. Explore its collections, exhibits, and educational programs to find out about the earth, and life and cultures.

Cat Tales
http://www.spokane.net/cattales/

Think cats have nine lives? Think again. Here, you'll discover why some of these skillful and graceful creatures are in danger of becoming extinct. See pictures of these big cats, learn what is causing their endangerment, and discover what you can do to help.

Cats! Wild to Mild
http://www.lam.mus.ca.us/cats/

This site follows the history of cats from exotic animal to favorite pet. You'll be surprised at just what your tame pet used to do!

Animals

Charlotte, the Vermont Whale
http://www.uvm.edu/whale/whalehome.html

In 1849, Vermont railroad workers made a bizarre discovery. They found fossils from a white whale. But what were fossils from an animal found only in Arctic waters doing in the middle of Vermont? Find out the complete story of this amazing discovery.

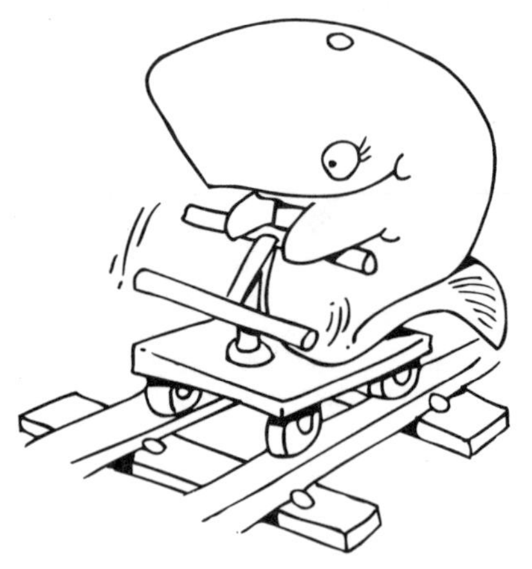

Chester Zoo
http://www.demon.co.uk/chesterzoo/

England's largest zoo is now open to the rest of the world. Take a virtual tour of its furry inhabitants and adopt your favorite endangered animal.

Children's Butterfly Site
http://www.mesc.usgs.gov/Butterfly.html

Get to know this miracle of nature through pictures, facts, and important butterfly questions like, "Where do butterflies go when it rains?" And don't forget to try creating your own butterfly.

Cincinnati Zoo & Botanical Garden
http://www.cincyzoo.org/

It's a zoo in here. The Cincinnati Zoo, to be exact. Packed with an art gallery, images, descriptions, and of course, your favorite furry, and not-so-furry, friends.

Crocodiles

http://www.pbs.org/wgbh/nova/crocs/

Find out about a creature that's been living on the earth for at least 240 million years. No, not the dinosaur—the crocodile. See how these reptilian kings outlived the dinosaurs to become some people's pets! But you just may think twice before taking one for a walk!

Curse of T. Rex

http://www.pbs.org/wgbh/nova/trex/

The dinosaurs weren't alone! Who else was here when the dinosaurs ruled the earth? Did they really rule? This PBS special reveals it all.

DINO-MITE Dinosaur Site

http://www.trib.com/DINO/

No other dinosaur site is quite as dino-mite! Featuring kids' art, stories, and poems, as well as questions about dinosaurs. A great place to share ideas and information about using dinosaur facts in the classroom.

Dinosaur: Interplanetary Gazette

http://www.dinosaur.org/frontpage.html

So, what do you want to know about dinosaurs? This is your subscription to everything dinosaur—from facts, pictures, cartoons, sounds, and videos to the latest happenings in the dinosaur world. Who said they're extinct?!

Animals

Dinosaur Reference Center
http://www.crl.com/~sarima/dinosaurs/

Tired of dinosaurs-by-the-number? Then get the true facts used every day by real-life paleontologists. If you've got a dinosaur question, this place has the answer—in an A-to-Z listing!

Dinosaur Valley Museum
http://www.mwc.mus.co.us/dinosaurs/index.htm

Think that dinosaurs don't still roam the earth? Think again. At a real paleontology laboratory (just big words meaning they study dinosaurs), they'll show you that dinosaurs are still around today. View exhibits, experiments, and even an expedition. No bones about it.

DINOSAURIA ON-LINE
http://www.dinosauria.com/

At this site, dinosaurs still roam the earth in all of their gigantic glory. Full of dinosaur collectibles.

Dinosaurs in Cyberspace: Dinolinks
http://www.ucmp.berkeley.edu/diapsids/dinolinks.html

Dinosaurs live! On the Internet anyway. One of the most comprehensive collections of Internet links to absolutely anything dinosaur. From fossils and exhibits to stories and clubs you can join.

Dog Fancy On-line
http://www.petchannel.com/dogs/default.asp

Dog names, dog companies, dog breeders, dog poetry, dog tributes, dog breeds, dog breeders, dog doctors, dog links, and dog games. Pretty much everything you could ever need or want for your dog.

THE DOG ZONE
http://www.dogzone.com/

Dogs, dogs, and more dogs. This site has tons of information on dogs: dog types, how to care for them, and products for your favorite pooch.

Dogz and Catz
http://www.dogz.com/

So you want a pet dog or cat but your parents don't? Well, now you can adopt your very own virtual pet. Try out a free demo.

Download-a-Dinosaur
http://www.rain.org/~philfear/download-a-dinosaur.html

Make your own dinosaur! If you have scissors, glue, and parental supervision, you can download paper designs to create and be overrun by your favorite dinosaurs. Just be careful of the raptors—they're looking at you a little funny.

Electronic Zoo

http://netvet.wustl.edu/e-zoo.htm

One of the very best sites on the Web for animal lovers. All the favorite domestic and wild animals are featured. Everything from household pets and farm animals to wild beasts are included in this big database of animals.

Endangered Species

http://www.nceet.snre.umich.edu/EndSpp/Endangered.html

Some of those cute playful animals that you love to love may not be around much longer. Why? Find out the numerous reasons and what you can do to stop your favorite furry friends from disappearing forever.

Endangered Species Home Page

http://www.fws.gov/~r9endspp/endspp.html

Did you know kids can make a difference in the life of an endangered animal? Get to know which animals are endangered, what causes this, and the power that kids like you have to save them. Contains games, puzzles, and tons of information and pictures.

Entomology for beginners

http://www.bos.nl/homes/bijlmakers/ento/begin.html

Think this'll bug ya? Entomolgy is the study of insects and, boy, is this site full of them! Discover how they grow up (called metamorphosis) and locate your favorite icky insect part.

EnviroLink
http://envirolink.org/arrs/gap/gaphome.html

Apes are people, too. At least that's what the Great Ape Project says—and they're not monkeying around. Help support the ape and fight for its rights while learning all about this hairy cousin of humans.

Extraordinary Dogs
http://www.wnet.org/extraordinarydogs/

PBS sponsors this site featuring dogs. Links to other dog sites, certificates for extra special achievements, and contests can be found here.

The FALCONS' NEST
http://www2.northstar.k12.ak.us/schools/upk/upk.home.html

Ever wonder what it would be like to live in Alaska? Now's your chance with this collection of little-known stories, facts, and photos by the students at University Park Elementary in Fairbanks, Alaska. Learn how a dog race is run, the finer skills of ice carving, and why moose walk around the school's playgrounds.

The Froggy Page
http://frog.simplenet.com/froggy/

Frog fun has gone hopping mad at this home for all kinds of virtual frogginess. Leap into frog pictures, songs, sounds, jokes, games, and stories. All right from your own pad.

!!!FROGLAND!!!

http://www.teleport.com/~dstroy/frogland.html

Do you know that it really can rain frogs? Strange and true facts are revealed here that will make you leap out of your seat. Fun facts, jokes, art, and everything froggy can be found at this site.

GeoZoo

http://www.geobop.com/geozoo/

If you're an animal, then you've found a home. If you're a person, well, they'll let you in, too. Go on safari through this huge collection of animal pictures, information, and links to your absolutely favorite animals.

Gordon's Entomological Home Page

http://www.ex.ac.uk/~gjlramel/welcome.html

Stop bugging people for information on bugs because here it is! This entire site is devoted to those creepy, crawly insects, spiders, centipedes, and more.

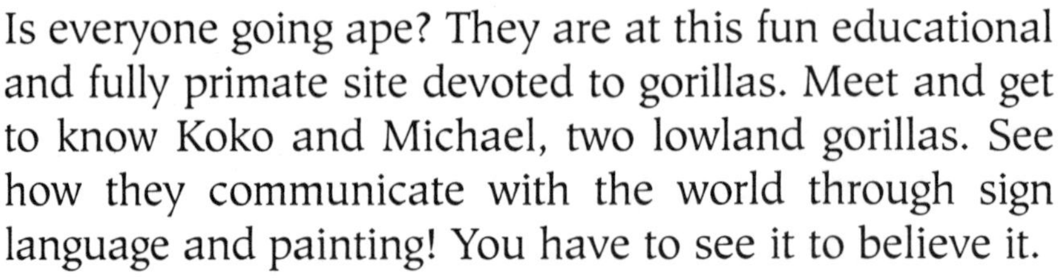

Gorilla Foundation Homepage

http://www.gorilla.org/index.html

Is everyone going ape? They are at this fun educational and fully primate site devoted to gorillas. Meet and get to know Koko and Michael, two lowland gorillas. See how they communicate with the world through sign language and painting! You have to see it to believe it.

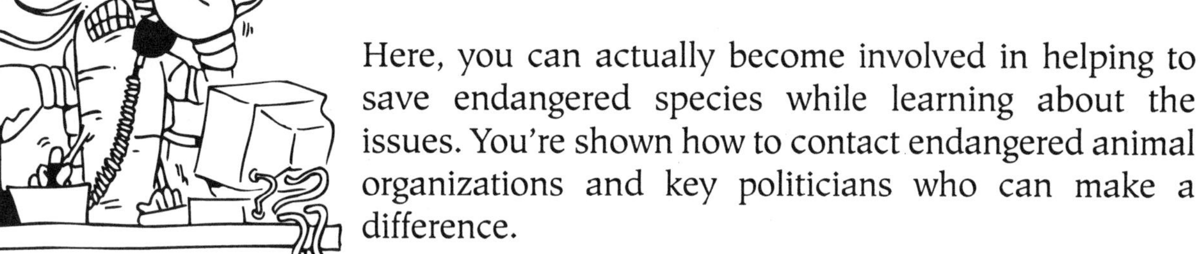

Habitat & Species: Internet Resources Collection
http://www.igc.org/igc/issues/habitats/

Here, you can actually become involved in helping to save endangered species while learning about the issues. You're shown how to contact endangered animal organizations and key politicians who can make a difference.

Honolulu Community College Dinosaur Exhibit
http://www.hcc.hawaii.edu/dinos/dinos.1.html

Dinosaurs on vacation?! Yep, dinosaurs are hitting the beaches, or at least Hawaii, in one of the finest and largest collections of dinosaur fossils in the world. And it's all on-line.

Horsefun Home Page
http://www.horsefun.com/

Horse lovers only should apply to this site. Get horse facts, read a "pony" tale, play with puzzles, enter contests, take a quiz, or just join the club. In fact, this site has everything but an actual horse.

Insect Drawings at Illinois
http://www.life.uiuc.edu/Entomology/insectgifs.html

Do you like to study creepy crawlies? If you can stand the "buggy grossness," the illustrations at this site are quite impressive and beautifully detailed.

Iowa State University Entomology Image Gallery

http://www.ent.iastate.edu/imagegallery/

This site wants to bug you. If it creeps and crawls, you can find information on it here—from beetles and flies to the "true bugs."

Kcarroll's Horse Country

http://www.horse-country.com/

This site isn't horsing around—on second thought, it is and in a big way. If you love horses, this site will gallop into your heart with information on these beautiful animals, including vet care, housing, racing, clothing, and absolutely everything you can do with a horse— even immortalizing it in art.

Kid's Korner at the Zoo

http://www.scz.org/kids.html

Do your parents say you belong in a zoo? Well, they're right. Especially here where you can go on a jungle adventure, run with the animals, play games, experience sights and sounds, and just be yourself.

King Cobra @ nationalgeographic.com

http://www.nationalgeographic.com/features/97/kingcobra/index-n.html

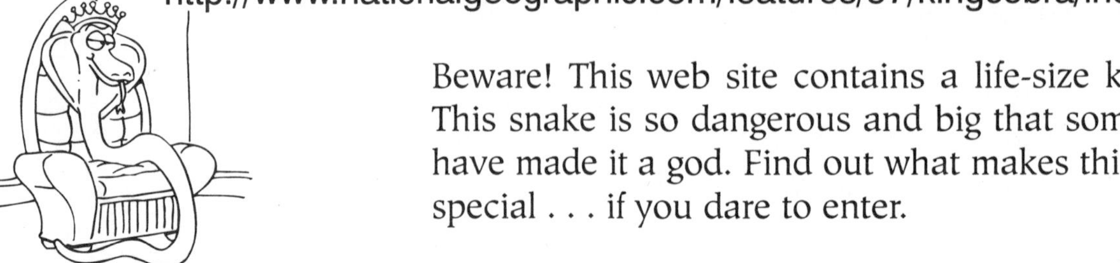

Beware! This web site contains a life-size king cobra. This snake is so dangerous and big that some cultures have made it a god. Find out what makes this snake so special . . . if you dare to enter.

▲▼▲

LlamaWeb

http://www.webcom.com/~degraham/

A whole lotta llama fun. Know what a llama is? Well, now you can know almost too much with llama history, facts, care, events, merchandise, and really, really fun llama stuff.

The Los Angeles Zoo

http://www.lazoo.org/

What contains 1,200 animals, 500 staff, 800 volunteers, and 40,000 members? The Los Angeles Zoo, of course. Whether you're doing a research project, planning an outing, or just looking for some wild fun, you'll find just what you need at the zoo.

The Marine World Theme Park

http://www.freerun.com/napavalley/outdoor/marinewo/marinewo.html

Home page to Marine World in California, this site offers pictures and information on the wonders of marine life and much, much more.

The Milwaukee County Zoo

http://www.execpc.com/Milwaukee_Zoo/

Can't make it to the zoo? Then, let the zoo come to you at this fun-filled, information-stuffed site dedicated to the Milwaukee Zoo. Includes animal movies.

Animals

NWF's Ranger Rick

http://www.igc.org/nwf/rrick/index.html

Ready for some outdoor adventure? You can become an official park ranger with access to colorful animal photos, exciting stories, cartoons, games, activities, and far-out animal facts. Why not start today with the outdoor activity of the month?

National Zoo Cinema

http://www.si.edu/organiza/museums/zoo/hilights/cinema.htm

Not satisfied just looking at pictures and reading about your favorite animals? Then view all of your favorite wild friends in full motion through this extensive library of animal movies. Better get the popcorn ready. (Just don't feed the animals.)

National Zoo Home Page

http://www.si.edu/natzoo/

Take a leisurely tour of the national zoo. Contains a photo library of all its furry inhabitants plus a history of the zoo. You can even set up a live video conference from your classroom.

Oakland Zoo Entrance

http://www.oaklandzoo.org/

Wish you could have a giraffe for your very own? How about a lion? Well, it's possible—sort of. You can view and read about your favorite animals, play games and activities, and even get a chance to adopt an animal for your very own.

Orcinus orca

http://www.slip.net/~oyafuso/orcinusorca/orca.html

What weighs 10 tons and travels up to 100 miles a day? Orca, the killer whale, of course. Get to know and understand these huge, yet docile and lovable, creatures of the sea. Filled with facts, photos, and fun.

Oregon Coast Aquarium

http://www.aquarium.org/

See life at sea level. Take a virtual tour of the Oregon coast and over 170 species of aquatic animals. See the famous star of *Free Willy*, Keiko, the killer whale. Talk with fellow fish lovers—all without touching a drop of water.

Oregon Zoo Official Web Site - Portland

http://www.zooregon.org/

Ever wonder how a rhino sees the world? Take a look through the rhino cam, stock up on those weird but true animal facts, and just go wild at Portland's zoo. Plus, learn how you can aid and support rhinos and other animals with 101 suggestions.

The Penguin Page

http://www.vni.net/~kwelch/penguins/

Put on your best tux and waddle into the ultimate penguin site. Everything you ever wanted to know about our feathered friends can be found here. Complete with in-depth info, real video, and a whole lotta penguins.

Animals

PetBunny Homepage

http://web.mit.edu/klund/www/bunny/bunny.html

A hare-raising experience. Learn about and share your love of rabbits at this informational site filled with bunny pictures, bunny care, bunny societies, and bunny newsgroups. Something bunny is definitely going on.

Photo Album

http://www.horses.co.uk/general/album.cgi

Ever wanted your own horse? Now, you can have pages upon pages of them in full brilliant color. This on-line photo album captures these magnificent steeds running, standing, and just horsing around. Print them to hang on your wall!

Pittsburgh Zoo - Kids' Kingdom

http://zoo.pgh.pa.us/kk.html

Now you can act like an animal and be praised for it! Get hands-on animal experiences with a kangaroo, otter, sea lion, and more, while the zoo keeper answers any questions you might have. You can't imagine the wild antics you can get yourself into here.

Primate Gallery

http://www.selu.com/~bio/PrimateGallery/

Wanna monkey around? Over 200 monkeys are waiting to swing with you. See videos, hear sounds, download color pictures, and even animate your favorite monkeys.

A Project by Lakeshore Elementary School 4th Graders

http://www.greeceny.com/ls/grade4/

While other fourth-grade classes were just reading about animals, at Lakeshore Elementary, they were creating them on their very own web site! See what kids like you know about animals. You can even view pictures they drew themselves. By kids for kids.

The Rainbow Raccoons

http://www.rainbowjoe.com/

These happy, colorful raccoons want to play with you and teach you about science, history, computers, and especially, fun. Explore, experiment, and make some new friends. Open your imagination.

Rattlesnake Ranch

http://www.wf.net/~snake/index.html

Snakes, snakes, and yes, more snakes. Slither around the famous Brazos River Rattlesnake Ranch as Bayou Bob tells you all about snakes, critical bite first aid, and the myths and folklore of the rattlesnake. Sink your fangs into games, contests, and free souvenirs!

San Diego Zoo

http://www.sandiegozoo.org/

Want to visit a zoo or are you feeling a little more wild? Well, now you can do both at the world-famous San Diego Zoo and Wild Animal Park. Get information on visiting, play games, send a virtual animal postcard, or just stop in to say "Hi" to your favorite animals.

Animals

San Francisco Zoo

http://www.sfzoo.com/html/map.html

Tour the San Francisco Zoo—virtually. Just click on a map to roam inside the lion house, swim with the sea lions, or play at the petting zoo. Full of colorful pictures and informational text on your favorite zoo residents. Worth the download time.

The Santa Ana Zoo

http://santaanazoo.org/

Monkey around at the world-famous Santa Ana Zoo. Take a private guided tour of your favorite furry friends or just take the zoo challenge to see if you have what it takes in the animal kingdom.

Save the Manatee Club

http://www.objectlinks.com/manatee/

What's a manatee? Manatees are big, cute, lovable animals that live in the sea. And unfortunately, they are in danger and need your help. Get to know one for yourself and find out just how you can help save an entire species.

Shark!

http://www.goodtech.co.uk/shark/

Help! A man fell overboard and you're his only hope. In this fun, yet challenging, on-line game you are a mermaid who must avoid sharks and other monsters of the sea to reach the drowning man in time. Are you up to the challenge?

Sounds of the World's Animals

http://www.georgetown.edu/cball/animals/animals.html

While animals make the same sounds around the world, each language expresses them differently. A "woof" is not always a "woof." For example, a dog from Sweden says "vov vov" while one from Japan says "won won." No kidding! Hear them for yourself when you listen to real audio clips.

The Tennessee Aquarium

http://www.tennis.org/

Want to see the largest freshwater aquarium in the world? Journey through a spectacular 60-foot canyon and 2 living forests, where you'll see over 9,000 animals that swim, fly, and crawl in their natural habitats.

Tiger Information Center

http://www.5tigers.org/

Have you ever wanted a tiger for a pet? Test your knowledge of these big cats and have all your tiger questions answered.

Turtle Trax - A Sea Turtle Page

http://www.turtles.org/

Make tracks to this great site that honors the wonder and beauty of the marine turtle. Learn why all species of marine turtles are either threatened or endangered. Full color photos, poems, and stories.

Animals

Virtual Dog Show
http://www.dogshow.com/

Enter your dog in a virtual dog show. Many categories from which to choose. Pictures are needed. Make your dog a star!

Virtual Frog Dissection Kit
http://george.lbl.gov/ITG.hm.pg.docs/dissect/info.html

Jump inside a frog to see just what makes it . . . well . . . jump. Using computer 3-D imaging and movies, you'll be able to view the entire anatomy of a frog from any angle you choose. A ribbit-ing experience.

Virtual Pet Home Page
http://www.virtualpet.com/vp/

The sun never sets on virtual pets—and this site proves it. For the newest products, research on future trends, and upcoming products, this is the information center for virtual pets. A virtual treat.

The Virtual Zoo
http://library.advanced.org/11922/

You've got a season pass to one of the biggest zoos on the Internet. This virtual zoo is filled with facts and pictures on all of your favorite animals. Slither past all of the on-line exhibits.

WWF for Kids

http://www.wwfcanada.org/wwfkids/index.html

Climb into an environmental tree house filled with wild animals and fun. Learn about endangered species and what you can do to help save them. You'll see how other kids have gotten involved and how easy it is. And don't be surprised if you find an adventure along the way.

Welcome to AntBoy's Bugworld!

http://www.heatersworld.com/bugworld/

Did you know that bugs are everywhere? Insects outnumber all other life on the planet. That's a lot of bugs and they all seem to be at this terrific site where you can find lots of buggy information, watch live ants build a colony, or link to the best bug sites of the Internet.

WELCOME TO ARABIAN WILDLIFE ONLINE

http://www.arabianwildlife.com/

Arabia's first wildlife magazine hits the Web in full, furry, reach-out-and-touch-it color. See the pictures of your favorite animals, animal web sites, and more.

Welcome to Healthy Pets

http://www.healthypet.com/index.html

No one wants your pet to be healthy and happy more than you do—except maybe the people behind this site. Learn how to keep your pet healthy, how to tell if it's not, and where to take it to get better.

Animals

Welcome to the New England Aquarium
http://www.neaq.org/

Want to watch a whale take flight on a helicopter? You can at one of the best educational, simple-to-navigate, and fun aquarium sites on the Internet. Complete with pictures, an on-line library, and fun at-home projects.

Welcome to the Oklahoma City Zoo
http://www.cpb.uokhsc.edu/okc/okczoo/zoomap.html

Where can you see 2,800 of the world's most exotic animals? In Oklahoma City, of course!

Whales' Songs
http://whales.ot.com/

Set sail aboard the *Song of the Whales* for a seafaring journey through the wondrous and mystical world of whales. Get a first-hand account of some of the world's largest mammals and come back with a whale of a tale to tell.

Whaletimes
http://www.whaletimes.org

The only place where you can ask a sea dog named Jake questions about dolphins, whales, sharks, and other sea-living creatures! Jake will actually reply to you with an answer to your questions while helping you write your very own stories about the ocean.

The Wild Ones
http://www.thewildones.org/

Rare and endangered animals hang, swim, and run wild here. View pictures and articles on each animal's history and conservation efforts, take part in interactive projects, and ask biology professionals from around the world your questions.

Wild Things
http://thingswild.com/

Think that there's only a handful of endangered species out there? Think again. The Nature Conservancy estimates that 22% of all vertebrates and 31% of all plant life are in danger of extinction. Unbelievable, huh? Check this site out for more.

Woodland Park Zoo
http://www.zoo.org/

See a world of nature here at Seattle's very own zoo. Woodland Park is waiting to take you on a virtual tour, display whimsical up-close photos, and answer any animal question you might have.

The World Wide Raccoon Web
http://www.loomcom.com/raccoons/

A raccoon that saved a college student's life? Read more tales about this black and white masked crusader, a sly and agile trickster who is too cute to miss.

The Worm Page

http://users.multiverse.com/~wibble/worm.html

A whole web site devoted to those icky, yucky, slimy, slinky things that creep and crawl. Learn about all the different types of worms and the important roles they play in the environment.

Zoocam.html

http://c.unclone.com/zoocam.html

Seeing spots? You will be if you visit this live Internet Giraffe Cam. Get to see your favorite spotted animals as they go about their daily zoo business. Updated every five minutes.

Zoom Dinosaurs - Enchanted Learning Software

http://www.EnchantedLearning.com/subjects/dinosaurs/

This site wrote the book on dinosaurs—literally. This on-line educational and entertainment guide is designed for students of all ages with an easy-to-use structure that offers just the information you would like. Why did the dinosaur cross the road?

ZooNet

http://www.mindspring.com/~zoonet

Want to visit a zoo? Pick and visit your favorite zoo from this extensive list or discover a new one. If there's a zoo out there, this place has it. (Unless, of course, it's your room.)

@rt_room

http://www.arts.ufl.edu/art/rt_room/@rtroom_home.html

A virtual learning environment for exploring the world of art. Choose from @rtrageous thinking, @rt sparkers, @rt gallery, @rt demos, and @rtifacts.

Academy of Achievement

http://www.achievement.org/autodoc/halls/art

Want to meet your favorite musician, actor, director, or writer? While it might not be face to face, these in-depth interviews, biographies, and video clips bring you so close to your favorite star that you could almost reach out and touch her or him.

All-Music Guide

http://www.allmusic.com/index.html

Have a favorite CD or movie? Looking for a new one? Find it here among thousands of reviewed and rated CDs and movies. Even includes credits and interesting facts.

The Animation ZONE - Tutorial

http://www.teleport.com/~chrisdb/taz/tutorial.htm

Are animated images running all over you? Then learn how to make and control these wonders of the Web with easy, simple-to-use instructions and tips. Your page will jump off the screen in no time—literally.

ART HISTORY RESOURCES
http://witcombe.bcpw.sbc.edu/ARTHLinks.html

Covering Prehistoric, Ancient Greek, Early Medieval, and many other important periods in art history, this database is a fantastic resource.

Art Resources
http://www.educationindex.com/art/

Looking for a favorite painting, museum, or artist? You'll find it here in this immense collection of links to everything art. See masterpieces up close, learn how to improve your techniques, or find out how gorillas are getting into the act.

ArtLex -- a dictionary of visual art
http://www.artlex.com/

Dictionaries aren't just for words anymore. This on-line dictionary of art is perfect for artists, students, and educators. You'll find definitions of over 2,400 art terms along with illustrations, pronunciations, notes, quotations, and links to other resources on the Web.

Aunt Annie's Crafts
http://www.auntannie.com

Aunt Annie has assembled an impressive list of ideas and directions for making interesting projects. Check her out once a week and you'll find a new craft suitable for both boys and girls.

Cartoon Corner
http://www.cartooncorner.com

What does a cartoonist do? How does a cartoonist draw? Well, here is the place to find out. Learn drawing tricks and have fun with your imagination!

Children's Music Web
http://www.childrensmusic.org/

Looking to put some music into your life? Sing, listen, create, and play music—all at this site. Talk about the music you love, hear what other people have to say, and just take some notes for yourself.

The Classical Music Pages
http://w3.rz-berlin.mpg.de/cmp/classmus.html

Search for information about music or composers according to the composer's name, instrument, the form, or epoch. Includes a glossary of musical terms and a short history of Western music.

The Cleveland Museum of Art
http://www.clemusart.com/

Stroll through more than 30,000 works of art from around the world that range over 5,000 years, from ancient Egypt to the present. Fun activities, photos, and facts will let you travel through ancient lands.

Color Matters

http://www.lava.net:80/~colorcom/

Did you know that color can affect the way you think, act, and react? Color can be a powerful weapon. Now, you can explore and learn just how to use it to get the results that you want—like that raise in your allowance, maybe?

Coloring.com

http://www.ravenna.com/coloring/

New images are always being added to this simple coloring book format. You can send your artwork through e-mail or print it out for the refrigerator.

The Comic Strip

http://www.unitedmedia.com/comics/

Many of your favorite cartoon characters have taken up a new residence on the Internet. New games, based on different comic strips, will keep you entertained for hours.

Cool Kids Gif Animation Art Gallery for Young Aspiring Artists

http://www.kaleidoscapes.com/current.html

Can you create graphic animations for the Web? Want to learn? Here, you can view what kids like you have created on their computers while trying your hand at creating your own animations.

craftcraze
http://www.geocities.com/Heartland/Plains/6474/cc.html

Projects you make from trash! Quick fix recipes! Rainy day projects for kids! A fun mix of good, wholesome stuff to do.

Crayola & Art Education
http://www.crayola.com/art_education/

Remember the awesome feeling of opening that gigantic fresh box of 128 Crayola crayons? Heavenly. Crayola still has that wonderful box of colors, but this web site offers a bit more. Lots of inspiring ideas on how to use art products.

Create-a-Saurus
http://www.adventure.com/kids/dinosaurs/createasaurus/

A commercial site with lots of goodies. You can design your own Tyrannosaurus rex by clicking on the outline, the colors, and the texture. Plus lots of other games!

The Cubist Coloring Book
http://www.webdiner.com/cubist/cubist.htm

Can't stay in the lines when coloring? Well, this is art where you don't stay in the lines—a cubist art coloring book. On these pages, you can print and color—any way you want.

▲▼▲▼▲▼▲▼▲▼▲▼▲▼▲▼▲▼▲▼▲▼▲▼▲▼▲▼▲▼▲▼▲▼▲▼▲▼▲

CyberKids Space
http://www.cyberkids.com

What's hot at Cyberkids? View multimedia theater, hear interviews with celebrities, read about young composers, and participate in an art and writing contest.

CYBERSPACE FILM SCHOOL
http://www.hollywoodu.com/

Has the film bug bitten you? Here you can learn how to produce a film, find an agent, contact a star, direct your first feature, and sell your script.

Draw and Color with Uncle Fred
http://www.unclefred.com

For over 60 years, Uncle Fred has been drawing the famous "Barney Google and Snuffy Smith" comic strip. On his web page, you can get some free drawing lessons from this master of his medium.

Eyeneer Music Archives
http://www.eyeneer.com

Hear sound samples. See illustrations of instruments. Look at Quick Time video clips. This site has a bit of everything for classical, contemporary, and jazz music lovers.

Greatest Films
http://www.filmsite.org/

Step into the movies. Seven decades of film are stored, here, with reviews, awards, quotes, posters, and downloadable video and audio clips. A film buff's dream!

H-GIG Historical Photographs Online
http://www.ucr.edu/h-gig/hist-art/photo.html

Photography has come a long way. Get to know the people behind this medium. Find out how photography came to be what it is and where it's going in this massive collection of links.

Idea Box-Crafts for Little Hands
http://www.intex.net/~dlester/pam/craft/craftlinkskids.html

A potpourri of craft projects and ideas. You can visit an enormous craft store on-line and get ideas on how to make gifts and holiday decorations.

Imagination Celebration
http://imagine.ppld.org/

Students, teachers, parents, artists, and yes, even your dog, can come here to share and learn about the visual and performing arts. Meet the people and places behind the art, see artworks for yourself, and even pick up some tips to make your own artworks.

The Impressionist
http://reality.sgi.com/employees/paul_asd/impression/09.html

Think you have what it takes to be a great painter from the impressionist school? Try your own hand (and computer mouse) at recreating the great impressionist masterpieces. Print out your works and show your friends!

Inside Art: An Art History Game
http://www.eduweb.com/insideart/index.html

An adventure in art history by Educational Web Adventures. Play this Art History game and discover how to recognize the world's greatest artists with just a few clues.

Jarea Kinder Art - free art lessons
http://www.bconnex.net/~jarea/lessons.htm

Over 160 free art lesson plans of every kind, including drawing, printmaking, painting, multicultural art, sculpture, and coloring pages. Features ways to cultivate creativity and an on-line kids' art gallery.

Joseph Wu's Origami Page
http://www.datt.co.jp/Origami

Once you see the paper creations assembled in this web site, you'll never look at a piece of paper in quite the same way again. Learn how to make a crane, a butterfly, a turtle, and more.

Kids' Film Festival of Virginia
http://members.aol.com/kidfilm/

This site features a film contest just for kids. If you think you've got what it takes, then visit Richmond, Virginia, via the Web and gain filmmaker status.

Kids Rule!
http://hukilau.com/kidsrule/

The Internet's best search engine and directory for kids' art sites. Picture lots and lots of goodies here.

Marilyn's Imagination Factory
http://users.hsonline.net/kidatart/

Trash as art?!! Yep, that bottle cap or old homework assignment can actually be put to good use as an airplane, kite, or even a dinosaur. Learn how you can recycle your everyday "trash" into fun and functional arts and crafts. You'll "refuse" to believe your eyes.

Miles of Styles
http://www.kn.pacbell.com/wired/art/styles.html

Painting is much more than just bowls of fruit and the *Mona Lisa.* Think you're a budding Picasso? Then try this fun activity to see how time and location influence a painting and the way you see it.

nFX Living Graphics
http://www.nfx.com/

Create your very own cartoons! You decide what your special character looks like and should be doing. Put it on display or talk it up in the chat room. Either way, something funny will definitely be happening.

100% Chillin'
http://home.ican.net/~703863/linzhome/

Send a digital card, listen to a jukebox, download free graphics for your web site, and go to the information zone.

Online Music Encyclopedia Homepage
http://library.advanced.org/10400/html/index.html

Absolutely everything you ever wanted to know about music. From the biographies of brilliant and misunderstood composers to the histories of the instruments they used—you'll learn it all. Complete with audio samples.

Photo Gallery
http://pathfinder.com/@@hCt0EAUArdwZpwuY/photo/gallery/home.html

If a picture says a thousand words then this site could fill a library. No matter what image you're seeking, you're guaranteed to find it here, in rich color or striking black and white.

The Piano Education Page
http://www.unm.edu/~loritaf/pnoedmn.html

Fans of the piano can access over 350 pages of information about the piano and music. Read an interview with musicians, get piano tips, and meet famous composers on-line.

Puppettools; The Internet Puppet Utility
http://www.puppetools.com/

Puppets aren't just for TV shows anymore. Now, puppets can be used to help you communicate in everyday life. Harness the power of puppets and learn how they can help you express yourself.

RCA: Idiot's Guide to Classical Music
http://www.rcavictor.com/rca/hits/idiots/cover.html

There's a lot more classical music out there than you'd imagine. Listen to music clips from shows and movies. The Idiot's Guide to Classical Music was designed for everyone.

RedFrog - "The Children's Art Gallery"
http://redfrog.norconnect.no/~cag/info.html

The gallery offers free exhibition space to kids who wish to present their drawings. Red Frog has created a platform where children, parents, and teachers can meet and share a part of their life experiences—captured in children's drawings.

The Refrigerator Art Contest

http://www.artcontest.com/

Get the thrill of exhibiting your very own artwork to hundreds of thousands of viewers. Enter your drawings in the weekly contest and you might be chosen.

Smithsonian Photographic Services Home Page

http://photo2.si.edu/index.html

Get the picture? A gigantic database of historic or just plain interesting photographs. They didn't stop there. Many unique features like "Offerings at the Wall," a poignant tribute to the legacy of Vietnam.

Stage Hand Puppets Activity Page

http://fox.nstn.ca/~puppets/activity.html

Make a puppet show. Get ideas for making your own puppets with simple materials found at home. Print out the patterns and add your own characters.

Sunshine Daydream: 360 Panoramic Pictures

http://www.sunshinedaydream.com/360degrees/index.html

Sometimes you need to see the ENTIRE picture. Breaking free from the limitations of photographs, this unique technology gives you a full 360-degree view of your favorite places in San Francisco. Now, you can really see what a city is like—every nook and cranny.

3-D Action Learning Homepage
http://www.actionlearn3d.com/

Download free demos. These three games use state-of-the-art graphics and stellar technology to captivate and entertain you while teaching grammar, history, and math skills. Learning has never been more fun.

3D riDDle - Home Page
http://cvs.anu.edu.au/andy/rid/riddle.html

Think you can solve a riddle? How about a riddle for your eyes? This site is packed with hundreds of pictures that contain hidden 3-D images. If you can see the image, then you'll know just where to go next to solve this puzzle. Up to the challenge?

3G on W3: The Great Globe Gallery
http://hum.amu.edu.pl/~zbzw/glob/glob1.htm

Go to outer space in your computer. Enter The Great Globe Gallery and take a journey with almost 200 pictures of our great globe from outer space.

3M Collaborative Invention Unit
http://mustang.coled.umn.edu/inventing/inventing.html

What makes an inventor successful? Learn just what it takes to become an inventor. Get tips and methods on how to bring success to your own inventions.

This Day in LIFE

http://pathfinder.com/@@e@el*gQAtHUIm5Cz/Life/thisday/thisday.html

This Day in LIFE lists interesting things that happened on today's date in many different years. Includes a collection of *Life* magazine covers. A truly fascinating journey through 20th-century history.

Timelines of Art History

http://www.dc.infi.net/~gunther/tl001.html

Did you know that just like you and me, art has a family tree that spans the globe? See how art grew over the ages from every corner of the world and how it evolved from primitive structures and cave paintings into what modern art museums display today.

ToonaCat's Kids Club, Creative Place for Kids

http://toonacat.com/

No admission or dues! An inventive kids' club where you can Ask a Super Sleuth, Write Stories, Print Designs to Color, and See Kids' Art.

Welcome to Piano on the Net '97

http://www.artdsm.com/music.html

A working composer and studio musician has created this site where Beginning, Intermediate, and even Advanced students can learn piano. Easy to follow. A piano keyboard is required.

World of Puppets
http://www.itdc.sbcss.k12.ca.us/curriculum/puppetry.html

Travel the globe to visit the bunraku puppet and all of Kermit's worldwide cousins to see how they're made and operated. Then, learn how to make a puppet for a puppet show of your very own.

World Wide Arts Resources -
Definitive Arts and Culture Information Gateway
http://wwar.com/default.html

If there is anything you want to know about art, you can find it, here. This massive art archive includes information on art history, art appreciation, museums, artists' biographies, and the various styles used throughout history.

World's Transportation Commission
Photograph Collection
http://lcweb2.loc.gov/ammem/wtc/wtchome.html

Ever wanted to travel around the world? How about in the 1890s? View hundreds of pictures that tell about a country, its people, and the culture at that time in history. Don't just read history—experience it.

AISP KidSpace Home Page
http://main.aisp.net/text/kid.htm

A list of links to commercial web sites, such as TazMania, Sega, Scholastic, and Toys 'Я' Us. You can also play game classics like Peg, Hangman, and PacMan.

Barfweb-Kids Only Page
http://www.barfweb.com/

Lots more good links to surf through. The general interest section contains some commercial stuff, but lots of game and chat areas. You can post messages on their Bulletin Board and visit places like Rome and Hawaii.

Bon Bevy Inc.
http://www.bonbevy.com/

Girls just want to have fun. And here, with the best crafts, poetry, art, short stories, and fun activities to be found on the Net, there's no more enjoyable place for a girl to be. Oh—boys can stop in, too.

Cool Central (TM)
http://www.coolcentral.com/

The hottest sites on the Web are cooled down for you. Get the best of the Web—sites that get the hits, not the pits. From sites of the moment to a sizzling, cool mystery adventure—you never know what you might find here . . . but it'll be cool.

Dodoland in Cyberspace
http://www.swifty.com/azatlan/

Over 2 million people from 60 different countries have visited this site. There's plenty to keep them coming back! Check out Giant Flower Island, a nature retreat, to learn more about the environment or go to Island of Eyes, a place to meet real authors and illustrators.

For Kids!

http://www.nwf.org/nwf/kids/index.html

The Animal Tracks Kids' Page has dozens of ways that you can "Take Action" to help endangered animals. Get a tour, play the games, or join the organization.

Free Zone for Kids

http://freezone.com/

Curiocity's Free Zone is part of the Curiocity family of products for kids which includes *Curiocity for Kids,* a monthly magazine, and *Curiocity's Brain Storm,* a weekly educational newspaper. You can chat, send e-mail, and play games.

GusTown: Fun

http://www.gustown.com/GusTown/Home/GusTownSummer.htm

Gustown has its own library, post office, toy store, museum, and cafe. Join Gustown's CyberClub. The Game Gallery, Cyberbud Kitchen, and Gustown Gazette all offer fun activities for you to do on-line.

Headbone Zone

http://www.headbone.com/

Price Buzz has free stuff and contests. Derby offers research adventures and Big Games will zap your brain with games to play.

Just for Kids - The Digby Awards
http://www.oh-no.com/kids2.html

Digby issues awards and badges to the very best web sites on the Internet that have been created by kids for kids. Don't miss this one!

Kid Sites
http://www.kidinfo.com/

After you've been through every site in this book, you can click here and find even more sites designed for kids and teachers. Almost every academic subject plus Hobbies and Games.

KidCity Intro Page
http://www.child.net/kidcity.htm

Window-shop at the Mall, travel to Planet X at the Spaceport, ride the coaster at the Amusement Park, or do some business at the Town Hall. Where can you do all of these things? Well, at KidCity, of course.

Kid's Corner
http://www.nbs.gov/features/kidscorner/

Color some of the rarest animals in the world . . . Endangered Species! A fun way to learn lots of things about animals that live throughout the world.

Kids' Corner: Rainforest Action Network

http://www.ran.org/ran/kids_action/index.html

Wonderful audio and visual help to let you know all about the great, large, and mysterious rain forests of the world.

Kids F.A.C.E. Homepage

http://www.kidsface.org/

Kids For A Clean Environment (Kids F.A.C.E.) is a children's environmental organization started in 1989 by a nine-year-old child. The club, with a current membership of over 300,000 worldwide, is dedicated to helping children learn more about the world in which they live and helping them to be more involved in the protection of nature.

The Kids' Place

http://www3.islandnet.com/~bedford/kids.html

What makes the colors in a rainbow? Why do they only occur when the sun is behind you? These questions and zillions more are answered at this fun site. Games, puzzles, and pictures about lots of subjects.

Kids Space

http://www.kids-space.org/

A simple idea. The site provides kids with pictures and themes every month. The kids then choose artwork or write a story that goes with the theme. Submit your creations, either music, drawings, or stories, and share them with a worldwide audience.

Clubs

MaMaMedia–Fun learning Activities for Kids
http://www.mamamedia.com/

Awesome, animated graphics take you to a variety of stories, games, and activities. Visit Cartoon Castles, Stamps and Stomps, and Presto Puzzles to start the fun.

Melpomene Institute: Special Girls Section
http://www.melpomene.org/girls.htm

Games and facts about girls and fitness. Divided into three age categories, there are interesting tidbits for girls of every age. Great links.

Rigby Kids' Places
http://www.reedbooks.com.au/rigby/kids/kidplace.html

Sites, sites, and more sites!! An extensive collection of sites of interest to kids from The Forces of Nature & Dinosaurs to Science, Space & Other Good Stuff.

Webcards
http://www.codysoft.com/webcards/

Just remembered that tomorrow is your friend's birthday? Just click onto Webcards and you can choose from hundreds of selections of cards for anniversaries, birthdays, illness, sympathy, and congratulations.

Welcome to GeoCities Enchanted Forest Neighborhood

http://www.geocities.com/EnchantedForest/

Princess Earsabelle and Prince Christofur invite you to visit The Castle in the Enchanted Forest. Here you will find special places to go, games to play, and stories to read.

Welcome to the Realist Wonder Society

http://www.wondersociety.com/

Many serious, thoughtful, and touching essays and short stories for children.

The Wonderful Wizard of Oz Website

http://www.eskimo.com/~tiktok/index.html

"It's not a place you can get to by a boat or a train. It's far, far away." These are words from The Wizard of Oz. This site is dedicated to everything Oz: A FAQ, biographical info on the original writers and subsequent writers, Oz memorabilia, and even how to write your own Oz book.

Bonus.com the SuperSite for Kids.

http://www.bonus.com

Educational quizzes and games. Lots of information for the budding genius.

The Computer Clubhouse

http://www.tcm.org/clubhouse/index.html

Divided into at least six different clubhouses, there's something of interest for everyone. Whether it's Brooklyn, Germany, or the Girl Scout organization, you'll have a chance to "travel" there.

Computer Lessons for Kids and Small Adults

http://www2.magmacom.com/~dsleeth/kids/lessons/starter.htm

How well do you know your computer? Maybe it's time you tamed your computer with these easy and fun lessons for kids and really small adults. Because the more you know about computers, the more fun they are.

Kids Domain

http://www.kidsdomain.com/

THE kids' computer site. Read reviews of software, download FREE programs and games, learn to program, build web pages, find teaching and parenting resources, and best of all, play on-line games, puzzles, crafts, and more. You will want to stay a kid forever.

Kids of the Web Main Frame Page

http://www.wenet.net/~leroyc/kidsweb/index.html

Kids created this site which consists of a list of sites on the web created by and for kids. Close to 500 pages are currently linked and you can "Adopt-a-page" by sending in your address.

Kidz Game Connection (Children's Educational Games)
http://www.crl.com/~colocomp/kidz.htm

Hundreds of games and educational software organized from A–Z. You'll never be bored again with so many programs. Free to download right onto your computer! Play Concentration with Egyptian hieroglyphics and get lost in a maze.

Kristy's Desktop Creations
http://www.kwebdesign.com/kdesk/

Want to add pictures and sounds to your computer? Don't have a clue how to do it? You could take an expensive computer graphics course or you could click onto this site. Kristy has compiled a bunch of graphics for you to download for free!

Aunt Edna's Kitchen
http://www.cei.net/~terry/auntedna/

There's always a goody to grab at Aunt Edna's Kitchen. Something is always cooking here. Tasty recipes with easy-to-follow instructions, nutrition tips, and real life cooking sounds. Soup's on!

Cooking with Kids
http://www.lightcooking.com/kids.html

It helps to know how to cook, if you want to be able to eat well. This site has great ideas for cooking. Fire up the grill!

Food & Nutrition

EatRight@CyberDiet.com - CyberDiet's Home Page
http://www.cyberdiet.com/

Want to live to a ripe old age? You know, like as old as your mom and dad? You remember the rules. Eat right and get plenty of exercise. Click on this site for hints on the "eat right" part.

Fitness Files Home Pages
http://fyiowa.webpoint.com/fitness/

Are you fit? You will be after getting the facts on exercise, healing, avoiding injuries, the coolest outdoor activities (for you and your friends), and fundamentals on fitness. A must for any athlete—or wannabe athlete.

International Children's Cookbook
http://www.b.shuttle.de/ml1000/cookbook.htm

A cookbook of delicious foods from around the world. Make sure you have an adult to supervise when you make some of these very wonderful foods yourself!

Kids Food CyberClub Home Page
http://www.kidsfood.org/

Parents can learn how to provide excellent nutrition. Teachers can get curriculum ideas and lesson plans on-line. This site features a clubhouse where grown-ups are politely requested to KEEP OUT!

Nutrition Cafe

http://exhibits.pacsci.org/nutrition/

Nutrition Cafe is where learning about what's good to eat is fun. Choose from games like Grab a Grape, Have a Bite, and the Nutrition Sleuth.

Pizza Recipes

http://soar.berkeley.edu/recipes/pizza/

Everyone loves pizza! All sorts of pizza recipes that kids can easily make. Be sure to have an adult around to supervise.

The Story of Milk

http://moomilk.com/tours/tour1-0.htm

Did you know that the average cow makes over 10 gallons of milk per day? Gallons?! Take a virtual tour through a dairy farm and see the process step by step. From the milking parlor through pasteurization, you'll never again think that milk just appears at the local grocery store.

Tossed Salad Productions

http://www.tossed-salad.com/

The Healthy Herb virtual playground invites you to learn about eating nutritiously, keeping your body healthy, and getting enough exercise. Play in their playground.

Food & Nutrition to Fun & Games

Welcome to KidsCandy!

http://www.kidscandy.org/

A great way to introduce kids to the kitchen. Who doesn't like candy? Here are recipes, tips, and secrets to making tasty treats.

ACE Kids

http://www.acekids.com/bkground.html

A great on-line starting place for your first web adventures. The Academic Center for Excellence has put together a list of safe links on the Web for kids, games, and educational activities.

The AIMS Puzzle Corner

http://www.aimsedu.org/Puzzle/PuzzleList.html

Puzzles for kids that help you learn. This site is written for teachers but the puzzles are for kids. Lots of different kinds to tickle your intellect and your funny bone.

ASL Fingerspelling

http://where.com/scott.net/asl/

Did you know that you can speak an entire language without saying a word? Learn how hearing impaired people communicate through sign language, speaking with their hands. Complete with a sign language dictionary and a quiz to see how well you can talk—so to speak.

The Adventurers
http://www.swp.com/adventurers/

The Adventurers is a series of stories about little folks known as, well, The Adventurers. Yes, they do have adventures. They get in trouble, battle the Grubby Gang, and have all of the appropriate lessons about the eternal pull between good and evil. You can even become your own "adventurer."

The Adventures of Superman and Batman
http://www.batman-superman.com/

Two of the most beloved superheroes come together in this powerhouse of a web site.

All Magic Guide
http://www.uelectric.com/allmagicguide.html

A guide to everything about the hobby and art of magic. Learn the secrets of the art and how you can become a magician.

BCPL Kid's Page
http://www.bcpl.lib.md.us/kidspage/kidspage.html

The Baltimore County Library special kids' page. Famous author interviews and lots of outside links. Ask questions about your favorite pets.

Fun & Games

Candy Stand

http://www.candystand.com/index1.htm

Games, games, and, . . . candy! Is your mind playing tricks or have you arrived at your dream site?! This candy stand serves up tons of interactive sports, card, and word video games as well as information on your favorite candies. There's never been a sweeter site.

CHARMAYNE's Kids' Stuff!

http://www.aracnet.com/~charmayn/kidstuf.html

From games and contests to submitting your own artwork and stories, this site has a bit of fun for any kid.

Chess is Fun

http://www.princeton.edu/~jedwards/cif/intro.html

A quick and easy way to learn how to play and win at chess. Reviews strategies, mind preparation, and tips for learning, winning, and mastering the game of chess.

Cool Dog Teddy's Home Page

http://www.fogbottom.com/morningwalk.html

Cool Dog Teddy contains stories designed for young children. Read the stories to your younger siblings or submit ideas for your own story.

Creative Matrix, Inc.
http://sandz.com/games/maze/

A completely a-maze-ing site. You are a famous adventurer in the Old West but your pal Winky Wink went looking for gold and got lost. Now, you're his only hope. Get him out! You can even create your own maze to stump your friends.

Cybercalifragilistic Greeting
http://www.webcom.com/~getagift/Birthday_Page.html

A creative way to send birthday greetings electronically without ever licking a postage stamp or shelling out $2.50 for a card. Many selections to choose from, some are even animated and have music!

DC Comics
http://www.dccomics.com

It's where Batman and Superman were born! DC Comics has been the birthplace of the world's greatest superheroes. You can visit them all at this site.

Dr. Bowen's Incredible Contest Club
http://www.contestclub.com/

CYBERTEAM ROOM! This is the place for games, contests, and links to other sites. Win stuff from Interplay, Playmates, Berserk, and more.

Dr. Toy's Guide: Information on Toys and Much More
http://www.drtoy.com/

Dr. Toy has given awards to over 500 toys or educational products. You can read full descriptions and find out where to get them.

4Kids
http://www.4kids.org/

Other than this great guide that you already have in your hands, how do you find fun and safe sites for kids on the Web? Right here, of course. An updated selection of the newest offerings for kids on the Internet.

Fleabusters' Kids Fun Page-Jokes
http://www.fleabuster.com/kids/kjokes.htm

Here's a whole slew of silly jokes for kids to use on anyone who will listen. See if you can stump your friends or family with these, sometimes corny, jokes.

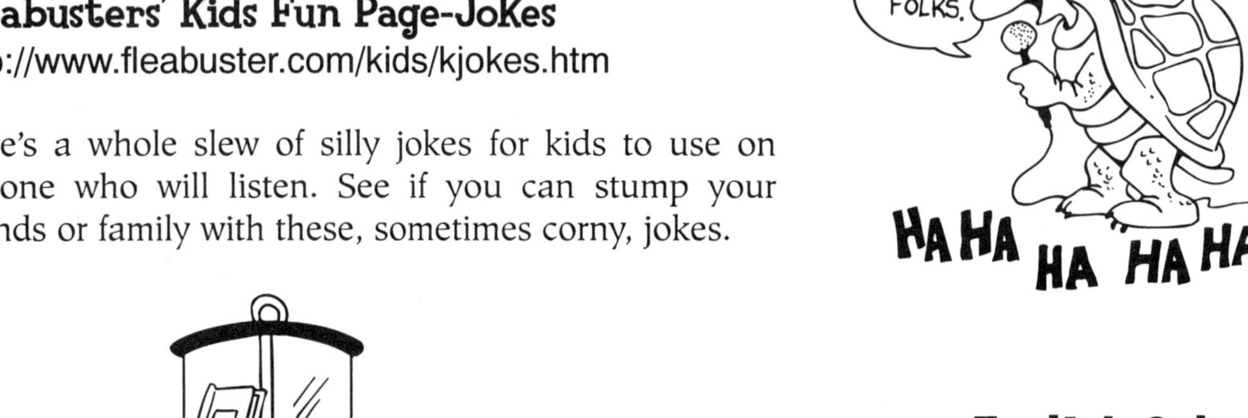

For Kids Only+
http://www.ci.berkeley.ca.us/bpl/kids/index.html

A great list of search engines to help you find what you want. Plus a directory of good books for kids. There's also a Homework Helper to answer some of those tough questions.

The Fun Centre!

http://www.interlog.com/~brucem/funcntr.html

Write a Story! Write a Song! Knock Knock Jokes! Play in the Game Room! Hear Riddles! A little bit of fun for everyone.

FUNHOUSE

http://www.imago.com.au/funhouse/

A funhouse with a literary bent! Meet the authors, read kids' stories, and enter your own short stories!

Games

http://www.cyberteens.com/games/Games.html

No downloading. No waiting. Just click and you're into some classic games. Only you don't need a game board or someone to play with. Just your computer screen.

The Games and Recreation Web Site

http://www.cis.ufl.edu/~thoth/library/recreation.html

Board games, card games, arcade games, table games, miniature-based games, and anything else you can think of with the word "game" attached to it can be found here.

Fun & Games

Gid's Blueberry Games
http://www.blueberry.co.uk/PIER-Gid.html

Nobody to play with? There's always someone to play with as long as you have a computer. This site features a whole slew of interactive computer games, like Mastermind and Webtris.

Good News Bears
http://www.ncsa.uiuc.edu/edu/rse/RSEyellow/gnb.html

Ever wonder what the stock market is? Introducing the Interactive Stock Market for grades K–12. A perfect way to learn the basics as well as more advanced ideas.

The Honey Expert
http://www.honey.com/kids/index.html

A honey lover tells you everything there is to know about making honey and the bees that do all the work.

Humongous Entertainment
http://www.humongous.com/

Fun can't get any bigger. This kid's playroom is chock-full of games, puzzles, coloring pages, and other fun activities!

KIDS FUN FOR ALL AGES
http://kidsfun.co.uk/

Pages to color. Ghost stories. And a place to put up your very own page. This site comes all the way from the United Kingdom.

KidSat Main Page
http://kidsat.jpl.nasa.gov/

Ever thought it might be fun to become an astronaut? NASA has sponsored this site to teach kids all about life in space.

KidsCom
http://www.kidscom.com/

Make New Friends, Cool Stuff, and Around the World are just a few of the places to explore at this fun site.

Kidz Game Connection (Children's Educational Games)
http://www.crl.com/~colocomp/kidz.htm

Hundreds of games and educational software organized from A–Z. You'll never be bored again with so many programs. Free to download right onto your computer! Play Concentration with Egyptian hieroglyphics and get lost in a maze.

The LaughIn Home Page

http://www.webpan.com/thelaughin/home.htm

Ready for lots of laughter, killer jokes, great poetry, a large collection of sound files, and helpful computer tips? Then leave your seriousness at the door and come on in to laugh yourself silly.

Magic Show

http://www.uelectric.com/magicshow

Hocus Pocus! Magic Show is an on-line magazine that features articles about professional magicians and their tricks. You can learn new tricks by watching the video clips and reading up on a magician's closely held secrets.

MANIC MAZE!

http://www.worldvillage.com/maze.htm

You are in for some a-maze-ing troubles. You awoke from a nightmare to find yourself trapped in a maze. You can't find your way out. Looks like the nightmare isn't over yet. Try to get out . . . if you can.

Marvel Universe On-line

http://www.marvelcomics.com/marvel.html

Silver Surfer, Ghost Rider, and the infamous Spiderman all live in the Marvel Comics universe. Trade cyber-cards, play games, and get a peak at new info on these characters.

Media Bridge-GameKids
http://www.gamekids.com/

GameKids allows you to download non-computer games, rhymes, activities, and recipes.

National Trust Kids' Site
http://www.trustkids.org/

Hunt and Seek, contests, activities, and other stuff to occupy yourself when you're sent to your room.

The Non-Stick MGM Cartoons Page
http://www.nonstick.com/mgm/

Tom and Jerry, Droopy, and all the other classic MGM characters can be found here with interesting tidbits of information about how they were created. You can download graphics and sounds of your favorite cartoon characters.

Not Just for Kids!
http://www.night.net/kids/

Rosie's Rhubarb Review has listed dozens of sites for kids. Well organized and pre-screened to avoid wasting time going to bad sites.

Fun & Games

OH! Kids

http://www.oplin.lib.oh.us/EDUCATE/

A site that specializes in collecting links of sites for kids that focus on fun. Hobbies, movies, games, and other fun-related sites are found here. Plus, a chance to visit Chocolate Town, U.S.A.

Peg Deluxe

http://www.onr.com/user/jeff/pegd3.htm

Are you ready to challenge one of the most addictive games around? Here, you can play the classic interactive video peg game that'll put your brains, intuition, and nerves to the test. Tons of levels and options to make each game more challenging than the last.

Pipsqueaks

http://www.childrensmusic.org/Pipsqueaks.html

Find out how to make your very own radio program. Listen to Pickleberry Pie, a radio show for kids. Check out what other kids are doing on the radio.

Professor Bubbles Official Bubble Homepage

http://bubbles.org

Get a secret recipe for making the best soap solution to blow colorful, long-lasting, and humongous bubbles. What is a Bubblesphere? You'll have to check this site to find out.

Rebound

http://www.raremedium.com/rebound/cmp/maingame.html

Think you're ready to go pro? Then grab that rebound and take it to the rim in this fully interactive basketball video game. You've got four chances to make the shots and win the game—but only if you have what it takes!

Rollercoasters

http://www.discovery.com/exp/rollercoasters/rollercoasters.html

If the roller coaster ride doesn't end when you leave the park, then this site is for you. Scream your way through video rides, pictures, rankings, polls, and even a chance to build your own thunderous coaster.

Sega Online: World Wide Soccer

http://www.sega.com/multimedia/games/soccer/

Wanna get your kicks? Try out your soccer skills on this fully interactive soccer game from Sega. It's up to you to kick the winning goal and only one thing stands in your way—the goalie.

Seuss Lorax Introduction

http://www.randomhouse.com/seussville/games/lorax/

Want to help save the world? Well, you're gonna have to do it one tree at a time. Play your part in this fun and fully interactive on-line video game that stars none other than Dr. Seuss's Lorax.

Fun & Games

Sherston Online

http://www.sherston.com/

Tired of the same few boring kids' software titles? Then come here to a world of kids' entertainment for the computer. For kids ages 3 to 16, these fun and educational games and programs will entertain, educate, and change your life.

Snowflake Attack

http://www.kaplan.com/holiday/snowattack.html

Oh no! You're being menaced by mutant snowflakes! Can you fight off these winter meanies without getting hit or running home to Mommy? The interactive video game that is the perfect antidote to holiday stress.

Toon Center

http://www.frontiernet.net/~jackson/

A doorway to your personal playground of original games, puzzles, stories, music, cartoons, and fun activities for kids of all ages. Just remember to wipe your feet on the mat.

Warner Brothers Kids

http://www.kids.warnerbrothers.com

Take a detailed tour of how a cartoon is created from the very beginning of an idea to the finished clip. From the home of Looney Tunes comes a great description of animation.

Web Battleship
http://gen.ml.org/battle/

The old Battleship game with tiny pegs is many decades old, but it has been given a new twist on the Web. Test your brains against the computer.

Webbie Web

http://www.kidland.com/netwrk.html

Hop on to the Web with this collection of kids' links that will let you play games, travel the world, and maybe even learn a thing or two. From family sites to pages that are for kids' eyes only!

Welcome to the Federation Role-Playing Game
http://youth.net/frpg/frpg.htm

Does the mention of *Star Trek* perk up your Vulcan ears? This Federation role-playing game will take you out of this world.

WonderKorner!
http://www.peak.org/~bonwritr/wonder11.htm

The Question and Answer Place for Curious Kids! Choose from a long list of questions to hear what other kids have asked. Submit your own question and, within days, an answer will be in your e-mail box.

Fun & Games to Health & Safety

WorldVillage
http://www.worldvillage.com/

Reviews, downloads, and games. Early childhood education. Live chat and even hobbies. Lots to do and lots to learn.

A World Wide Web For Kidz - fun and games for kids
http://www.4kidz.com/

The themes change weekly, but one thing stays the same: games and puzzles that are a blast to play.

clickable pyramid
http://www.nal.usda.gov:8001/py/pmap.htm

Don't know what to eat? You will when this food guide pyramid shows you just what your body needs daily for good nutrition. Discover the proper variety of foods that will provide the nutrients and calories you need to maintain a healthy body.

FEMA for KIDS Homepage
http://www.fema.gov/kids/

The Federal Emergency Management Agency (FEMA) will teach you just what causes disasters and how to prepare your family for one. It offers games and real stories from kids who've been through actual disasters.

Healthy Choices for Kids Online
http://www.healthychoices.org/

Wait! Is your snack healthy for you? Get the nitty-gritty details on your food through information and fun activities. Find out why the saying "You are what you eat" really rings true.

KID SAFETY on the INTERNET - The Police Notebook
http://www.ou.edu/oupd/kidsafe/start.htm

A fun and interactive slide show will quiz you on whether you know how to protect yourself and handle emergencies like a pro.

A Kids Eye Safety Guide
http://www.optima-hyper.com/kidsafe.htm

Take a safety quiz to learn how to protect your eyes from injury and possible blindness. Each quiz page has a button for free coloring pages with cool eye trivia.

My 8 Rules for Safety
http://www.discribe.ca/childfind/educate/8tips.hte

Do you know how to be safe? The National Center for Missing and Exploited Children has developed this site to remind kids of important ways to keep safe, both in real life and on the Internet. And you can start with just eight simple steps.

NCADI: For Kids Only
http://www.health.org/kidsarea/index.htm

Do you know how to say no to drugs? Wally Bear and all his friends do and they are ready to show you how. Get the facts, in English or Spanish.

National Crime Prevention Council On-line Resource Center
http://www.ncpc.org/

All about McGruff and Scruff, the two safety characters. Effective programs and self-help sections.

Safe Kids Home Page
http://www.safekids.com/

The World Wide Web can be a big and scary place. Learn how to stay safe on the Internet with these great tips for kids and teens.

Safe-T-Child On-line
http://www.yellodyno.com/

Learn how to be safe and trick those tricky people through educational words, songs, games, and fun-filled activities. With Yello Dyno's secret powers, you'll be in control.

Safety Bear's Coloring Book

http://www.dps.state.ak.us:80/AST/safety/safebear.htm

No one knows safety like Safety Bear and Safety Cub do. And they know that learning safety means having fun—especially with a coloring book, games, and stories with their friends, Scruff and McGruff.

Smokey Says

http://www.smokeybear.com

Only you can prevent forest fires! Smokey is still sending the message of how to handle fire safely, but now he's interactive with games to help you remember those important safety tips.

Vince & Larry's Safety City

http://www.nhtsa.dot.gov/kids/

Dummies really know a lot. Let the crash test dummies take you on a guided safety tour. They'll visit all the greatest safety spots where you'll play some games, see a movie, and realize that you can learn a lot from a dummy.

Welcome to the Vita-Men!

http://www.vita-men.com/

The superhero team of Vita-Men need your help to battle the forces that threaten your health. Supporters of health, preventers of disease, and protectors of your cells—vitamins are the heroes that your body can't do without. These super nutrients will take you up, up, and away.

Alexander the Great

http://spidey.cs.rit.edu/~bvs4997/faq/13.3.html

What the heck made Alexander so great and why, after 1,000 years, are people still talking about him? Everything you ever wanted to know about the greatest military ruler of all time—including his mysterious death.

Amber, A View of The Past

http://kadets.d20.co.edu/~lundberg/amber.html

If you want to still be here in another 30 million years, just go and find some sap from a tree and get embedded in it. That was the premise of the *Jurassic Park* movie and it's the theme of this web site.

America's West - Development & History

http://www.AmericanWest.com/

This site celebrates the pioneering American spirit. It traces the development and expansion of the Wild West and also takes a look at today's Modern West.

ARMAMENTARIUM: the Book of Roman Arms and Armour

http://www.ncl.ac.uk/~nantiq/arma/

This is an on-line book of Roman arms and armor. Complete with photographs and illustrations, you can get a real feel for the way that the early Romans went to war.

Betsy Ross

http://www.libertynet.org/iha/betsy/

Take a virtual tour through Betsy Ross's famous house in Philadelphia where she is believed to have sewn the very first United States flag in 1776. Learn about the controversies. Did she really sew it? Who designed it? Learn the secret art of cutting a perfect five-pointed star.

Black History

http://www.kn.pacbell.com/wired/BHM/hunt.html

Test your knowledge of Black History. Search the Web to find answers to questions. See if you can locate enough answers to conquer the "Big Question."

Blackbeard

http://www.geocities.com/Athens/7012/blackbeardinfo.html

Avast, ye maties! Beware all those who enter this site, the home of history's most infamous pirate, Blackbeard. Do you dare to find the facts and myths of the pirate who captured more than 45 ships in his lifetime?

Castles on the Web

http://fox.nstn.ca/~tmonk/castle/castle.html

Take a tour through the world's greatest castles. Read comments from people who've actually visited them!

Daily Life in Ancient Civilizations

http://members.aol.com/Donnclass/indexlife.html

Visit Ancient Rome, Ancient Greece, Ancient India, Ancient Egypt, and, if that isn't enough, Ancient China. Learn the mysteries of these old cultures and the richness they bring to modern life.

Exhibits Collection–The Middle Ages

http://www.learner.org/exhibits/middleages/

In the movies, life in the Middle Ages is portrayed as heroic and romantic. In reality, it was harsh, dangerous, and brutal. Plagues wiped out entire towns. Take a closer look at what life in Medieval times was really like.

Explorers of the World

http://www.bham.wednet.edu/explore.htm

Learn about the types of people who would give up the comforts of home for a life of exploration. Find out what it takes to be the kind of person who faces challenges for the thrills of discovery and exploration.

1492 Exhibit

http://sunsite.unc.edu/expo/1492.exhibit/Intro.html

This on-line exhibition examines what happened between the first visitors to North America and the native peoples already living there. What did they think of each other? What did they do?

Flints and Stones
http://www.ncl.ac.uk/~nantiq/menu.html

This on-line exhibition takes you on a journey into the lives of the Stone Age hunters and gatherers. People survived totally on what the land and sea could give them.

Historic Mile
http://www.libertynet.org:80/iha/virtual.html

Did you know that there are over 65 historic places to see within one mile in Philadelphia? Come on a journey through one of the first cities in America's history.

HistoryEgyptology.com
http://www.egyptology.com

Examine the art, archaeology, history, and religion of Ancient Egypt. Walk like an Egyptian!

The HistoryNet Archives - Great Battles
http://www.thehistorynet.com/THNarchives/GreatBattles/

It has been said that history is really the study of war. This site archives the Great Battles of the world's wars.

The History Place Presents Abraham Lincoln

http://www.historyplace.com/lincoln/index.html

Abraham Lincoln is most famous for ending the Civil War and abolishing slavery. He accomplished even more during his presidency. Find a great biography on Honest Abe.

Is the Past in Your Future?

http://www.sha.org/sha_kbro.htm

An archaeologist to me is Indiana Jones running from a two-ton boulder chasing him through a cave. Actually, there is a bit more to it. This site tells you about an archaeologist's work and why it might be a fun career for you.

Leonardo Home Page

http://www.mos.org/sln/Leonardo/LeoHomePage.html

Leonardo Da Vinci. Explore the life and times of one of the world's greatest painters, scientists, and inventors.

LibertyOnline Home Page

http://libertyonline.hypermall.com/

A complete collection of important American founding documents like the Constitution and a series of thought-provoking lectures from Aristotle to Abraham Lincoln are all to be found at this site.

MLK Page

http://www.wmich.edu/politics/mlk/

See a time line of the American Civil Rights movement. Gain a deeper understanding of the issues that Martin Luther King, Jr., stood for in this informative look at his life and times.

MSU Vincent Voice Library–President's Page

http://web.msu.edu/vincent/presidents.html

Listen to Vice President Lyndon Johnson react to the news of John F. Kennedy's assassination. Listen in on Richard Nixon's farewell speech. These are just a few examples of the sound clips of Presidents' speeches you can listen to at this site.

The Mayflower Web Pages

http://members.aol.com/calebj/mayflower.html

See how important the *Mayflower* is to American history. Find out about the people it carried, the laws it inspired, and the facts and myths that surround this vessel.

A Moment In Time

http://www.amomentintime.com/

A Moment in Time is a two-minute historical presentation that reaches 200,000 people a day. It makes history come alive with great sound clips and a theatrical format.

Monticello, Home of Thomas Jefferson

http://www.monticello.org/

A detailed examination of one of the most famous American Presidents. He was called a "miser with his time." Here you can see just how he spent some of that time.

Mysterious Mummies

http://www.pbs.org/wgbh/nova/chinamum/

A mummy is, simply put, an old dead body. Somehow it's been preserved. What you get is a dead person that still has some tissue, skin, and, certainly, its bones. Kind of creepy, huh?

The Original Titanic Page

http://gil.ipswichcity.qld.gov.au/~dalgarry

The best place to read about the unsinkable ship that sank. Loads of interesting details, ranging from the way the ship was built to the amount of food aboard.

PIRATES

http://www.nationalgeographic.com/modules/pirates/maina.html

National Geographic has designed a colorful site on pirates. Great photographs and stories about these infamous outlaws of the sea.

Ravensworld: The Titanic Web Site Introduction

http://www.ravens.net/titanic/titanic.htm

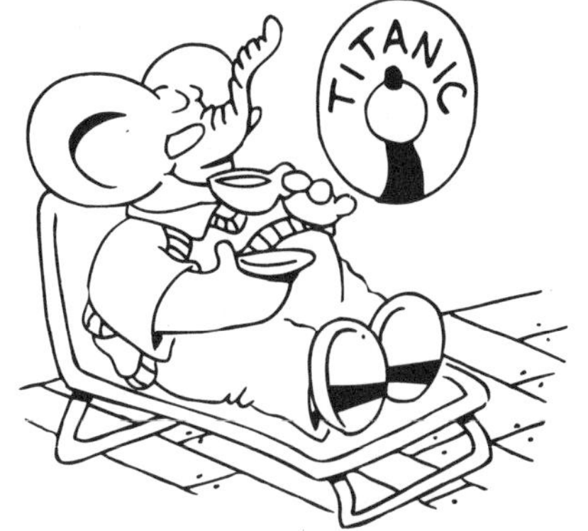

Take a tour of the *Titanic*. Read about the people aboard this maiden voyage of an "unsinkable" ship. Find out the mysteries and myths behind the *Titanic*.

THE ROBIN HOOD PROJECT
at the UNIVERSITY OF ROCHESTER

http://rodent.lib.rochester.edu/camelot/rh/rhhome.htm

The Robin Hood Project is a database of images, text, bibliographies, and stories about Robin Hood. Other web links to Robin Hood tales included.

Steam Trains

http://www.retroweb.com/steamtrains.html

For decades, the old steam locomotives moved cargo and people across America's vast frontier. Download photographs and hear the legends of these old work-horses.

Stewart Wright's Paleo Page . . .
http://www.GEB.com/net/sw.html

What's in a bone? Well, at Stewart Wright's paleontology page, you can learn about this unusual science and why it's worth digging into it.

Titanic - Raising a Legend On-line

http://www.discovery.com/area/science/titanic/titanicopener.html

Exclusive photographs of the real *Titanic* are available at this site. Watch film crews, explorers, and scientists as they search for clues about the *Titanic's* infamous voyage.

The Underground Railroad

http://www.cr.nps.gov/delta/under.htm

The Underground Railroad was a secret revolt against the evils of slavery. This site honors the heroes as it chronicles the evolution of this important period in American history.

The Viking Network Web

http://viking.no/

Get to know what it was like to be a Viking. Here you can participate in ongoing projects that are happening right now.

A Walking Tour of Plimoth Plantation

http://spirit.lib.uconn.edu/ArchNet/Topical/Historic/Plimoth/Plimoth.html

Plimoth Plantation is a living history museum that recreates 17th-century life in New England. Actors in period clothing are working, farming, and doing their daily activities.

WELCOME TO ARCHIVING EARLY AMERICA
http://earlyamerica.com/

Sparkling Commentary! Profound Questions! Brilliant Answers! Here, you enter the world of Early America. Participate in activities such as joining the conversation at The Town Crier.

Welcome to Webcorp Multimedia!
http://www.webcorp.com/civilrights/index.htm

History comes alive through the sights and sounds of yesteryear. Hear firsthand just what great leaders and figures of history had to say.

Yo, ho, ho
http://whyfiles.news.wisc.edu/036pirates/queen_annes_revenge.html

Arrggghh! Here, there be pirates. But more specifically, here is history's most famous pirate ship. Explore what is rumored to be the remains of Blackbeard's 100-foot ship, the *Queen Anne's Revenge,* and the possible treasure that it holds.

The Amazing Body Pavilion
http://www.mhms.org/amazing.html

Houston's Museum of Health and Medical Science has an interactive exhibit that actually walks you right through the human body. Naturally, it's only a photo simulation. You've got to go to Houston to walk through the real thing.

Human Body

Anatomy

http://rpisun1.mda.uth.tmc.edu/se/anatomy

Here, you'll see the skeleton as well as many other body parts. Divided into six areas; you select the one on which you wish to focus.

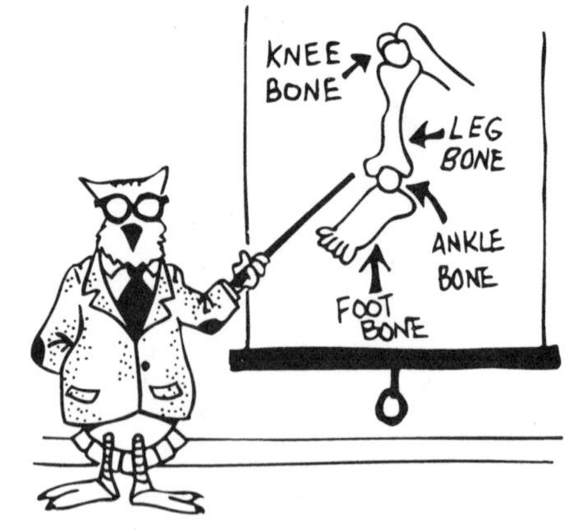

Anatomy of the Eye

http://www.eyenet.org/public/anatomy/anatomy.html

The American Academy of Opthamalogy has designed a nice site that includes the anatomy of the eye, eye safety, myths, and a quiz section.

Body Atlas

http://www.bluecares.com/good/body/

An atlas of the body. No need to buy expensive software of the human body. It's all here in living color. Sometimes yucky but interesting all the time.

CELLS alive!

http://www.cellsalive.com/

Incredible resources for budding scientists interested in those microscopic cells and the viruses, bacteria, and other bugs that plague them.

HealthNET - Welcome to the virtual Health-Net (From CPG/UK)

http://www.healthnet.org.uk/main.html

Kevin and Sean want to show you how to eat well, exercise right, and be in the know when it comes to your health. And, if you're feeling up to it, they may just play a game or two with you.

The Heart: An Online Exploration

http://sln.fi.edu/biosci/heart.html

The Franklin Institute in Philadelphia has long been famous for its gigantic walk-through replica of a human heart. Now, on-line, you can discover interesting things about the human heart.

How Your Brain Really Works

http://quest.arc.nasa.gov/neuron/events/baw/

Without our brains, well, we wouldn't be able to use our computers or even read this guide for that matter. What goes on inside our gray matter really matters. This site enlightens us all.

Human Anatomy On-line - InnerBody.com

http://www.innerbody.com/indexbody.html

Understand what's under your skin. Lots of bones and muscles and veins and . . . well, you get the picture. A virtual encyclopedia of information.

Aunty Math

http://www.dcmrats.org/AuntyMath.html

So, you can add faster than a calculator and out-multiply a rabbit. But are you up for a challenge that will test every math skill you've ever learned? How about tackling a new one each week?!! It's math gone wild.

Department of Treasury Learning Vault

http://www.treas.gov/opc/opc0034.html

Did you know that every day, 22.5 million dollars is printed in paper currency? The Department of the Treasury will tell you anything you've ever wanted to know about money—except, of course, how to get a whole lot of it.

Grade 1 Frame

http://www.accessone.com/inew/grade1Frame.htm

Your own private math tutor awaits you. Learn how to add, subtract, figure out time and money, and even try your hand at a word problem. Math has never been easier.

Grade 3 Frame

http://www.accessone.com/inew/grade3Frame.htm

Practice activities and lessons in mathematics for third and fourth graders. Younger math whizzes are welcome to try.

Kids Bank

http://www.kidsbank.com/

Did you know that banks do more than just store your money? Go on an interactive journey with Penny, Interest Ray, Mr. Money, and the entire gang as they show you just what happens to your money before and after you hand it to the bank teller.

Kids' Money Kids' Page

http://pages.prodigy.com/kidsmoney/kids.htm

Got money problems? Well, if you had come here first, you wouldn't. Find out how to stretch that meager allowance by determining what you should be doing with it. You'll be telling your parents how to manage their money in no time.

Look Who's Footing the Bill

http://www.kn.pacbell.com/wired/democracy/debtquest.html

Did you know that the United States has a trillion dollar debt? Do you know who has to pay for it? You! (Wow! That's a lot of allowances!) Better learn how to fix it. America's future rests in your hands.

Math Baseball

http://www.gold-pages.com/math/

Take a swing at math problems with this fun and challenging combination of baseball and math. It's the bottom of the ninth and it's up to you to win the game by solving addition, subtraction, multiplication, and more. Play math!

Math

Mathemagic Activities

http://www.scri.fsu.edu/~dennisl/CMS/activity/math_magic.html

What happens when you try to mix math and magic? A whole lot of fun. Like, learning card tricks that involve fundamental mathematical principles. For anyone who has ever thought math was boring.

Money

http://www.aplusmath.com/cgi-bin/flashcards/money

So, you think you could out-bank a banker? See just how good your money-counting abilities are with these fun and (cover your ears) educational money quizzes.

Money Curriculum Unit

http://woodrow.mpls.frb.fed.us/econed/curric/money.html

Everyone needs and uses money. Whether you are learning to spend your allowance wisely or starting a small business raking the neighbor's leaves, this site can help you learn how to manage money properly.

Money Talk

http://www.sys.virginia.edu/~wwwle/jun/module.html

Money, money, and yes, more money. Learn how to determine the value and appearance of money, what your money is worth in Japan and other foreign countries, and how to correctly count up your own allowance.

Paper Money
http://www.wco.com/~chappell/

Stamps aren't the only thing people collect. Did you know that people collect money, too? See how a money collector views money from around the world. Who knows? That dollar bill may be worth a little bit more than you thought. And you thought money was just good for spending.

Sovereign Bank Presents: KidsBank.Com!
http://www.kidsbank.com/

This site says it's a fun place for kids to learn about banking and money. And it is!! A great site by a commercial bank where you can explore and explore.

Welcome to Lemonade Stand
http://www.littlejason.com/lemonade/index.html

It's never too early to learn how to make money. This classic game for young entrepreneurs is great on-line.

Willoughby Home
http://Schoolcentral.com/Willoughby/default.htm

Math becomes magical when Merlin the Wizard teaches you your math facts. Math has never been easier to learn—or so out of this world.

Math to Pen Pals

World Paper Money

http://aes.iupui.edu/rwise/

Ever thought of holding onto your money instead of spending it for a change? How about for a lot of change? Get tips on how you can start a money collection and see what money looks like in virtually every country in the world.

CPAW Computer Pals Across the World

http://reach.ucf.edu/~cpaw/

Computer Pals Across the World bridge time and distance by letting you and your school communicate and share your experiences, ideas, and knowledge with educational and community institutions all over the globe.

International Kids' Space

http://plaza.interport.net/kids_space

Meet new friends from around the world as you share stories and artwork. In a section called Kids' World Village, you can find kids' home pages that are organized by category.

It's Our Pen Pal Spectacular!

http://www.agirlsworld.com/geri/penpal/index.html

A great site to send and receive messages from pen pals all over the world. Sorry, boys. This one's for girls only.

KidsConnect: AskKC

http://www.ala.org/ICONN/AskKC.html

If you are looking for some great ideas or need answers, this is the place for you. A helpful librarian will refer you to the right resources.

Welcome to FriendNet

http://www.mindspring.com/~rlackey/kids.htm

On-line games and free digital postcards. This is the place to meet on-line pen pals from all over the world. Get your e-mail out and start writing!

The Academy of Natural Sciences

http://www.acnatsci.org/

Two great categories at this site are Butterflies and Dinosaurs. Also check out Know Your Environment, Birds of North America, Scientific Research, and Traveling Exhibits.

Atmospheric Optical Effects

http://covis.atmos.uiuc.edu/guide/optics/html/optics.html

Sunlight and moonlight interact in ways that create amazing optical effects. See photographs and learn how these effects are created.

Planet Earth

Cyber Jacques' Cyber Seas Treasure Hunt
http://www.cyberjacques.com/

Fish and plants and mammals. Do a tile puzzle or play a tangram game. You won't even notice you are learning all about life in the deep blue sea.

Desert Life
http://www.desertusa.com/life.html

Desert Life in America's Southwest is a great introduction to the ecosystem of the desert. Learn about the important roles that humans play in the life of the desert.

Destination: Himalayas - Where Earth Meets Sky
http://library.advanced.org/10131/

Take a once-in-a-lifetime journey to the world's highest mountain chain, the Himalayas. Representing the awe-inspiring power, beauty, and grandeur of nature, the Himalayas are waiting to take you on a guided tour while offering real-life stories of adventurers who have conquered and been conquered by these majestic wonders.

Earth Alert
http://www.discovery.com/news/earthalert/earthalert.html

Did you know that our planet is in constant turmoil? At this moment, a tornado could be devastating a town across the world. Get to know just what disasters are changing the face of the earth.

Earth Day Young People's Resource Center
http://www.cam.org/~cdsl_ps/Earth_Day/earthday.htm

Earth Day has become a tradition. Every year since 1970, the United States has set aside one day to remind ourselves of the beauty and fragility of the earth. This list of resources will help you to find a way to get involved.

Earth Force
http://www.fi.edu/earth/

If you've ever felt the rumble of an earthquake or seen the eruption of a volcano, then you've witnessed earth force. Venture underground to see the turbulent forces that push and pull the earth to cause eruptions, quakes, and floods.

Exhibits Collection–Garbage
http://www.learner.org/exhibits/garbage/intro.html

Did you know that the average American creates about 1,570 pounds of trash a year? Get to know all the trashy details and what you can do to save our planet at a site that is devoted entirely to garbage.

Explorers Club
http://www.epa.gov/kids/

The Environmental Protection Agency has put together a web site to help kids think of ways they can work to save the environment.

Planet Earth

Fantastic Y E L L O W S T O N E

http://www.nationalgeographic.com/modules/yellowstone/index.html

Yellowstone National Park is one of the most famous parks in the world. *National Geographic* has produced a great web site that allows you to "Catch a Geyser" and "Plumb the Depths."

4-H Page

http://aggie-horticulture.tamu.edu/kinder/sgardens2.html

Where does soil come from? 4-H has been around for decades answering these and many other questions for kids. This web site introduces you to water, air, and soil through on-line games and activities.

Give Water A Hand

http://www.uwex.edu/erc/

Did you know that some people have to walk two miles just to get a gallon of water? This page explores the scarcity of this essential human requirement and the ways that we can help to conserve it.

Glacier

http://www.glacier.rice.edu/

Better put on some extra layers because Antarctica is the coldest, highest, driest, windiest place on earth—and you're about to step right in the middle of it! Learn why Antarctica holds the earth's life in its hands. Ice sold separately.

Glaciers and the Glacial Ages

http://www.uvm.edu/whale/GlaciersGlacialAges.html

Glaciers affect our mountains, rivers, and lakes. See photographs and learn how they are formed at this site.

Global Warming: Focus on the Future

http://www.envirolink.org/orgs/edf/

Want to get heated up? The message, here: Global warming is happening. Global warming is real. What is global warming exactly? Find out at this site.

Great Plant Escape

http://www.aces.uiuc.edu/uplink/gpe/

Here's a chance for some real growth! Help Detective Le Plant and his partners, Bud and Sprout, unlock the amazing mysteries of plant life.

Imagine The Universe!

http://imagine.gsfc.nasa.gov/

What is actually known about the universe? How is it evolving? Scientists discuss the universe and the mysteries that currently have them baffled.

Planet Earth

The Journey North

http://ics.soe.umich.edu/JourneyNorth/IAPHome.html

This web site explores three themes: the environment, wildlife migration, and different cultures. Students share their observations on wildlife migration and read about other kids' reports.

Kids front page

http://www.1800cleanup.org/kidpage.htm

Help Handy Andy keep the world clean. Tips for easier recycling. How to conserve the world's most precious resources. Learn how to make a difference in your own community and your own home.

KinderGARDEN

http://aggie-horticulture.tamu.edu/kinder/index.html

Do you like growing plants? Games, puzzles, and advice on how kids can plant, grow, and harvest a beautiful garden.

Life in the Ocean

http://encarta.msn.com/schoolhouse/oceans/oceans.asp

Microsoft network has created a beautiful and thorough site on Life in the Ocean. See a cross section of the ocean that shows marine organisms.

Map Machine: Atlas @ nationalgeographic.com
http://www.nationalgeographic.com/resources/ngo/maps/atlas/index.html

You will never find so many maps in one spot. A great place to start a trip or look at the far corners of the world. Lots of wonderful images and information.

Mapmaker, Mapmaker, Make Me a Map
http://loki.ur.utk.edu/ut2kids/maps/maps.html

Geography helps us know where we fit in our world. Maps help us get there. You'll see all kinds of maps and learn all about them.

Meteorology A to Z
http://www.nwlink.com/~wxdude/topics.html

A is for atmosphere. B is for big, burning sun. C is for condensation. The list continues. A weather song from the weather dude plus links to weather sites.

Myst@RainForests-"Where there is a Balance"
http://www.geocities.com/RainForest/Vines/1009/

Gain knowledge about the plants and animals of the rain forest. Tour the tropical rain forest. Learn about web sites and people who are taking action.

Planet Earth

Ocean Planet

http://seawifs.gsfc.nasa.gov/ocean_planet.html

Bet you didn't know that gigantic green forests grow in the deep blue sea? Creatures of the sea abound in these lush forests. Learn about some of them at this interesting site.

PLANET EARTH HOME PAGE -- Everything

http://www.tidusa.com/PEHP2000/Planet_Earth/map001.htm

Take care of your mother, Mother Earth, that is. The earth is vast and wide and deep and long and needs everyone to help out. Find out how, when, and where.

The Rain Forest Primer

http://www.coe.usu.edu/eb/northamerica/rainforestprimer.html

You might not think that the rain forest actually impacts almost every living being on this planet. It does. This site tells you how and why and what you can do to help save the rain forest.

Rainforest Tour

http://www.pbs.org/tal/costa_rica/rainwalk.html

PBS has created a virtual guided tour through a rain forest. See the monkeys and apes swinging from the vines, learn what foods and medicines come from the rain forest, and find out why they are endangered.

Secrets.Sea
http://www.secretsatsea.org/

Tracking down ocean pollution is no easy task. It takes keen observation, a deep understanding of the sea, and an ability to piece together clues in order to crack the code. Think you can master marine science in this interactive game?

Seeds of Change Garden
http://horizon.nmsu.edu/garden/

Everyone eats. Everywhere in the world, people need to eat. This site explores eating habits from all over the globe. Delicious recipes, ways to grow your garden, and an on-line adventure are all part of this unique site.

Seeds of Life
http://versicolores.ca/SeedsOfLife/home.html

All living things come from seeds in one way or another. This imaginative site covers everything about seeds, the very beginning of life.

Taking care of our planet page
http://www.cotf.edu/ete/starthere/takecare/takecare.html

Time to learn about caring for the earth! There are lots of things that we all can do to preserve the natural resources of the world. Preserve the earth.

Understanding Earthquakes
http://www.crustal.ucsb.edu/ics/understanding/

Earthquakes are nothing to take lightly. Look at a rotating globe of recent earthquakes. Take a quiz to test your knowledge of earthquakes. Read accounts of earthquakes and see how they start.

Volcano World
http://volcano.und.nodak.edu/vw.html

This site simply erupts with information. Ever thought of becoming a volcanologist? Here, you'll find lessons and activities that will teach you about volcanoes.

Water Works
http://www.omsi.edu/sln/ww/waterworks.htm

Water is everywhere, but what is water and how does it work? Investigate fountains. How do they work? How do they squirt in different directions?

Welcome to Earth's 911
http://www.1800cleanup.org/

Help Handy Andy keep the world clean. This site has tips for easier recycling and conserving the world's most precious resources. Learn how to make a difference in your own community and home.

Welcome to Geo-Globe: Interactive Geography!

http://library.advanced.org/10157/

If you want to know about world geography, this is the right place for you! Find out the answers to "How deep is the ocean?" and "What's the world's largest waterfall?"

Welcome to the Audubon Institute Web Site

http://www.auduboninstitute.org/

The earth's most fascinating habitats are explored at this site. Visit rain forests, swamps, undersea environments, and much more.

Welcome to the Wildlife Conservation Society

http://www.wcs.org/

Dedicated to conserving wildlife everywhere, this organization has a variety of activities which are geared to teach you about the dangers that animals face.

Why Is the Ocean Salty?

http://www.ci.pacifica.ca.us/NATURAL/SALTY/salty.html

From where did the salt in the ocean come? Can we drink ocean water? How much is there? Why do we have to conserve water if there is so much of it? These questions and many more are answered at this web site.

Planet Earth to Reading & Writing

The Wonderful World of Trees
http://www.domtar.com/arbre/english/

Trees, trees, and more trees. There's more to the world of trees than meets the eye and it's all here at this Canadian site.

Wonders of the Seas
http://www.oceanicresearch.org/lesson.html

Go get your cnidarian and echinoderm. No, those aren't typos. They're animals. They, and others like them, are featured at this site of strange and unusual animals.

Wyland Kids Web
http://www.wylandkids.com/

This site is dedicated to all the kids who care about saving the Planet Ocean. At Wyland Kids' Web, they believe that one kid can truly make a difference and they give you lots of ideas on how.

The Adventure
http://www.banph.com/Menu.shtml

Have the adventure of your life in this futuristic medieval world where insects rule the earth and humans no longer exist. The Adventures of Banph are the tales of an unlucky ant knight's endeavors to defend his kingdom against enemies of the Carpenter Empire. Will he succeed?

The Adventures of Earth Dog: Page 1
http://www.earthdog.com/story/page1.html

Ever dreamt of having superpowers that enabled you to save the world? Ever thought you'd be a dog? Environmental superhero Earth Dog needs your help to change the world for the better. Join his team and help him decide where he should go next in his courageous and colorfully illustrated adventures.

The Adventures of Hip-O
http://www.explorer.com.sg/hip-o/

Have fun with Hip-O, the hippiest purple hippopotamus in town! Travel the world with this wacky hippo as he teaches you interesting facts, ways to stay healthy, and how to care for the environment. Don't forget about the prizes.

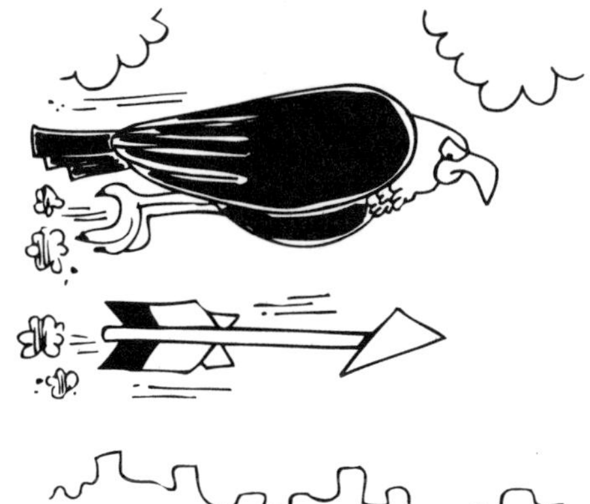

Aesop's Fables
http://www.pacificnet.net/~johnr/aesop/

You'll have your hands full with this on-line collection of over 600 fables, complete with audio narrations.

Bab's Online Stories
http://amtexpo.com/babbooks/index.shtml

This site is filled with the best bedtime stories you'll ever read. What? Not enough? Then try your hand at writing your own silly story.

Billy Bear's Animated Storybooks
http://www.billybear4kids.com

Finally, a place where kids can be kids. Billy Bear is waiting to play with you. Free fun and games, storybooks, songs, pictures, and even a place to create your own story. Just watch out for mud pies.

The BookWire Reading Room
http://www.bookwire.com/links/readingroom/readingroom.html

Sure, reading is fundamental but, here, it's also free! You choose from hundreds of your favorite and future favorite books. Print them out or read them right on-line. The choice is yours.

CANDLELIGHT STORIES - Children's Stories
http://www.CandlelightStories.com/testnav.htm

Curl up with a good book—right on-line. Hundreds of illustrated bedtime stories that you'll love. Complete with games and a section to submit your own illustrated stories.

Children and Youth: Table of Contents
http://www.ncpc.org/child.htm

Activities and information to read on a variety of subjects. Start a Neighborhood Watch, learn Street Smarts, or play the "What If" game.

Children's Stories, Poems, Pictures and Sounds

http://www.comlab.ox.ac.uk/oucl/users/jonathan.bowen/children.html

Looking for someplace to go? Well, here's your map to more stories, pictures, poems, and sounds than you could ever imagine. Includes links to games and other fabulous places.

Creative Writing for Kids – Welcome from The Mining Company

http://kidswriting.miningco.com/

You get to write your very own story. Filled with step-by-step instructions and helpful links.

CyberBee

http://www.cyberbee.com/

Look up in the sky. It's a bird. It's a plane. No, it's CyberBee. CyberBee has been as busy as a bee collecting Internet treasures just for you. Learn how to make a web page, send a CyberBee postcard, or, travel to the Web's funnest and most educational sites. Un-bee-lievable!

CyberSeuss

http://www.afn.org/~afn15301/drseuss.html

Is that a whocket in your pocket? No, it's the great and glorious Dr. Seuss! This world of CyberSeuss brings you unpublished stories, quizzes that could stump a grinch, and more activities, pictures, and sights than you could shake a woontoozle at. Explore, enjoy, and, as always, imagine.

Reading & Writing

The Fluency Through Fables Index
http://www.comenius.com/fable/complete.html

Was the tortoise really faster than the hare? Find out the truth behind this and other well-known favorite fables through fun and educational exercises.

Grammar Rock
http://genxtvland.simplenet.com/SchoolHouseRock/grammar.hts?lo

"Conjunction Junction, what's your function?" Sing along with all those favorite Saturday morning School House Rock songs as you learn about nouns, verbs, and interjections. Play the songs, read the lyrics, and watch the actual videos!

Grandpa Tucker's Rhymes and Tales
http://www.night.net/tucker/

There's always a smile awaiting you, here. With silly poems, funny stories, and amusing pictures, Grandpa Tucker will keep you laughing.

Hercules
http://www.perseus.tufts.edu/Hercules/

Ever wondered what it would be like to be a hero? How about Greece's greatest hero ever? Hercules will entertain you with his stories of heroic adventures, great battles, and romantic loves.

Inez Ramsey's Kids Sites
http://falcon.jmu.edu/~ramseyil/kids.htm

A great listing of links to all kinds of interesting sites for kids. Start with her section on Activities and Game. Go to Arts and Crafts and to Meet Authors. Check out Cowboys and the Wild West.

KABUKI for EVERYONE
http://www.fix.co.jp/kabuki/

Kabuki is a traditional form of Japanese theater that's been around for over 300 years. View actual plays and illustrations, listen to music, and go behind the scenes.

Kid Pub WWW Publishing
http://www.kidpub.org/kidpub/

At Kid Pub you can find over 18,000 stories written by kids from all over the planet. Read your favorite story, create your own, or just find a pen pal to keep you company. Here kids are always "write"!

theKids.com: Tales to Tell
http://www.thekids.com/kids/stories/

From nonsense rhymes and fables to adventure stories and imaginative tales. Colorful pictures pop off the page and make you feel like you're right there in the story. When you're done reading, play games or write about your own favorite story.

The Kids' Storytelling Club

http://www.storycraft.com/

Do you know where to go after "Once upon a time"? This interactive web site will teach you how to come up with an idea, create a story, and tell it in a manner that's fun and easy to understand. Your story is guaranteed to live happily ever after.

Korean Folk Tales

http://www.lg.co.kr/public_html/index2.html

You don't have to speak Korean to enjoy these whimsically animated Korean folktales. Complete with optional narration, these entertaining tales each have a message that is up to you to figure out—if you're not too busy with the coloring book and games.

Look Learn and Do

http://www.looklearnanddo.com/

Look Learn and Do allows you to do just that: look at great books, learn interesting history and facts, and do fun-filled projects with easy-to-follow, illustrated plans. Fun for the whole family.

The Magic School Bus Fun Place

http://place.scholastic.com/magicschoolbus/index.htm

In this magically transformable bus, a wacky science teacher named Ms. Frizzle takes you along with her class of enthusiastic, inquisitive students and her playful sidekick, Liz, the lizard. Educational and fun field trips packed with games and activities. It's the ride of your life.

Reading & Writing

National Geographic On-line

www.nationalgeographic.com

Features from the television program are beautifully translated onto this web site. Exquisite photographs, trivia quizzes, and brain teasers are all here. Just click on the passport to begin your journey.

OWLkids Online

http://www.owl.on.ca/

This monthly on-line magazine offers great categories for kids. Check out the Comic Adventures of the Mighty Mites, the World of Science from A–Z, and the Joke Zone.

Positively Poetry

http://advicom.net/~e-media/kv/poetry1.html

Created by kids for kids, this rhyming site has a mood that's just right. Read poems from around the world by kids just like you or try your own hand at writing a poem that could be read by the entire planet!

Read Room

http://www.readroom.com/

When you read a book, you can travel anywhere. Start here, with tons of books for you to learn about almost any place. Or, if you get homesick, just hang around, learn how to make a TV show, and do a few fun activities.

Reading & Writing

Romanian Fairy Tales

http://www.geocities.com/Athens/Delphi/2896/

Tired of hearing the same old fairy tales over and over again? Well, here are some amazing tales that have been hidden for centuries in the "old country." Pick any one of these fantastic, yet traditional, Romanian fairy tales for the story of your life.

SafeSurf Kid's Wave

http://www.safesurf.com/kidswave.htm

Great places to take kids on-line. SafeSurf is a system that rates web sites and is very helpful, especially when you are new to the Web.

Seminole County Public Library System - Kids' Page

http://www.co.seminole.fl.us/comsrvs/library/kids/

From Animals to Zoos, this librarian has gathered educational sites categorized by subject.

Snow White

http://www.scils.rutgers.edu/special/kay/snowwhite.html

Think you know the story of Snow White? Think again. Stored here are the story and images of Snow White along with studies into one of the most fascinating fairy tales ever told.

Stone Soup Magazine
http://www.stonesoup.com/

This on-line magazine is professionally done. It contains stories, poems, and artwork from kids around the globe.

Stories for Scouts
http://www.macscouter.com/Stories/index.html

Those campfire stories don't have to die out with the fire. Keep them "alight" with this immense story collection that contains humor, morality, ghosts, and mystery. Even submit your own favorites.

Treasure Island - Home
http://www.ukoln.ac.uk/services/treasure/

Beware of dastardly pirates while you hunt for buried treasure amidst a tropical setting. The book *Treasure Island* comes to life with everything you ever wanted to know about the author, characters, and the story. Explore the island, design your own pirate, and hunt for treasure. Avast, maties!

Welcome to DreamBox
http://www.dreambox.com/storybox/storybox.htm

Surprise lurks behind every corner at StoryBox. Enchanting illustrations will take you on a magical journey with stories that unlock your imagination. Be a pirate, play with your favorite bear, or fly wherever the wind may take you.

Reading & Writing to Science

Welcome to KidStory
http://www.kidstory.com/

KidStory is a fun and exciting place to enjoy stories and poetry created by kids just like you. You can even have your very own stories and pictures placed here, play interactive games, or just let your imagination run wild. After all, here, kids rule.

Welcome to Kino's Storytime
http://www.pbs.org/kcet/storytime/

Storytime breaks out of your TV and onto the Web with Kino and his collection of favorite illustrated stories, tips for making reading more fun, coloring sheets, games, and videos.

Welcome to Weekly Reader Galaxy!
http://www.weeklyreader.com/

Neatly broken up into all the elementary-level brackets, this magazine covers science topics that are interesting for kids.

Activities and Demonstrations
http://teacherlink.ed.usu.edu/nasa/rockets/activities/activities.html

Bored on a rainy day? Then follow these easy directions to make a few fun scientific "experiments." From bottle rockets to an antacid tablet race.

Alexander Graham Bell's Path to the Telephone–Home Page

http://jefferson.village.virginia.edu/albell/homepage.html

Bet you've used the telephone a lot. But remember, there was a time when no one had a telephone. Follow the adventure of inventing the telephone and learn lots and lots of exciting details.

AT THE FARM

http://miksike.com/unit/

Old McDonald's farm was nothing like this! Take an interactive journey with Margarita as she discovers everything there is to know about living on a farm— from pig farming to crop cultivation. You'll be wearing suspenders and a straw hat in no time.

Attack of the Killer Germs

http://tqd.advanced.org/3361/

A site put together by students about viruses and the paths of destruction they can cause.

Ask Dr. Science

http://www.drscience.com/

Ask Dr. Science some burning science questions, such as: "Why do so many scientists have beards?" This comical know-it-all will give you all the answers to science that you want to know—and even some that you don't!

Bill Nye on Magnetism

http:nyelabs.kcts.org/nyeverse/episode/e21.html

Bill Nye is that wacky science guy on TV. Here, he demonstrates how to make a compass with only a bowl of water and a needle. At the same time, he manages to teach us some basic principles of magnetism!

Bill Nye the Science Guy's Demo of the Day

http://apps.disney.com/DisneyTelevision/BillNye/demoday.cgi

You never know what's cooking in Bill's lab. Visit this site every day for a new and interesting science project. Connect to the Science Guy's U-Nye-Verse for more fun with science.

Boeing 727

http://www.networks.net/community/msd/727.htm

Ever wondered what it would be like to fly a Boeing 727 airplane? Take a virtual tour of this mighty aircraft that will have you buckling up for flight.

Build-It-Yourself

http://northshore.shore.net/~biy/

Trade ideas with inventors from around the world! Download free top-secret plans for building something awesome. Watch animations of how to make your contraptions move.

Children, Science for Kids, Projects & Experiments
http://www.waterw.com/~science/kids.html

Science fun for children and science help for adults. Science in the news and many more categories.

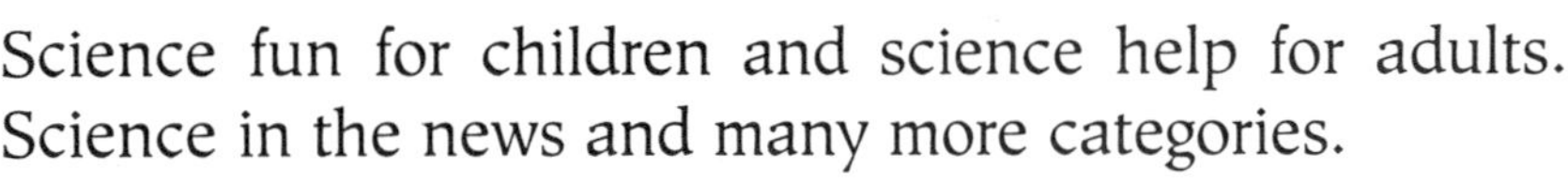

Dragonfly
http://miavx1.acs.muohio.edu/~dragonfly/

The *Dragonfly* magazine is for investigators of any age. All you need in order to join is your thinking cap and some questions in your pocket.

EXPERIMENTAL SCIENCE PROJECTS:
An Introductory Level Guide
http://www.isd77.k12.mn.us/resources/cf/SciProjIntro.html

From Observations and Information Gathering to Hypothesis and Conclusions, this site goes over the fundamentals of scientific experimentation.

Explore Science - Interactive Science Education
http://www.explorescience.com/

A site designed so that you can interact with material on the Web rather than just read the words on a page. An impressive series of modules featuring different aspects of science.

EXPLORIT SCIENCE CENTER
http://www.dcn.davis.ca.us/go/explorit/

Explorit is a hands-on science center for people of all ages. Check out the monthly science quizzes. Join the Astronomy Club.

The Eye
http://KidsHealth.org/parent/healthy/eyeshock.html

Seeing is believing—but how in the world do your eyes see? Go on an interactive slide show that explains blink-by-blink how you see the world. You won't believe your eyes.

Faster Than Sound
http://www.pbs.org/wgbh/nova/barrier/

How fast can you go? Fifty years ago, test pilot Chuck Yeager traveled faster than sound. Now, he'll let you in on some secrets. See the fastest vehicles in the world, read facts and stories on breaking the sound barrier, and find out what the heck a sonic boom is.

Fight BAC!
http://www.fightbac.org/

Do you know just what you're eating? Be careful—you may be eating bacteria. Find out just what this microscopic bug can do to you and how you can stop it.

Fireworks Safety

http://www.fireworks-safety.com/plate.main/forkids.html

Help America's life-safety superhero, The Preventor, battle misconceptions about fireworks. Read his comic book story, see what happens when good kids play dangerous games, and join The Preventor's team by learning how to use fireworks safely.

Floating & Sinking

http://www.pbs.org/wgbh/nova/balloon/science/density/

Imagine balloons filling the sky as they go up, up, and away—and then ask yourself why they aren't falling down, down, and going splat. Discover just what makes a balloon float as you go on a virtual balloon flight.

From Windmills to Whirligigs

http://www.smm.org/sln/vollis/

Did you know that the wind can power an entire city? See just what the power of the wind can do in the Vollis's family yard and how you can harness this power with your own experiments at home. You might just be blown away.

Get A Grip on Robotics

http://www.thetech.org/hyper/robots/teaser/

Ever shake a robot's hand? You will want to after you find out how robots are "lending a hand" to perform jobs and tasks that humans couldn't do. See how robots are changing our economy, health, knowledge, and the world in which we live.

Science

▲▼▲

How Light Works
http://pen1.pen.k12.va.us:80/Anthology/Div/Albemarle/Schools/MurrayElem/Instructional Resources/Light/How_Light_Works.html

This site explains how light works. A downloadable version is even better than the on-line one.

I Want To Be A Veterinarian
http://vet.futurescan.com/vet/index.html

Do you want to be a vet? This site can answer all of your questions and maybe some you hadn't even thought of as of yet.

Invention Dimension
http://web.mit.edu/invent

It's all about inventions. You get biographies of famous inventors. You get accidental inventions. You get not-so-famous inventors of famous inventions.

The MAD Scientist Network
http://medinfo.wustl.edu/~ysp/MSN/

A goofy, yet intelligent, site on science. At this site, they are out to prove that science and scientists can be wacky and fun.

   "

Mr. Warner's Cool Science!

http://home.unicom.net/~warnerr/

A science teacher has put together a thoughtful site that covers many facets of science. He has an on-line curriculum, teacher resources, science celebrities, and interviews.

Museum of Science and Industry Exhibits

http://www.msichicago.org/exhibit/exhome.html

A simply great collection of on-line exhibits. From hatching chicks to the Apollo 13 mission to the moon, there is something interesting to see. Guaranteed, you'll keep coming back for more.

NPR Science Friday Kids Connection

http://www.npr.org/programs/sfkids/

Welcome to Science Friday. Fill out a survey. Go behind the scenes and learn a lot about science.

Nature and Science

http://www.microweb.com/nature/index.html

Discover the world. Animals, rocks, clouds, and bugs! Why do leaves fall and flowers bloom? Why do animals hide and birds migrate? Answers to questions like these abound at this site.

Nova Online: Kaboom!
http://www.pbs.org/wgbh/nova/kaboom/

Think fireworks are all fun and games? See how fireworks do what they do and how they can, literally, bring down the house.

OMSI – Science Whatzit
http://www.omsi.edu/online/whatzit/home.html

Here's where you can find answers to your science questions—the really hard ones that you thought couldn't be answered.

Pyrotechnics: The Art of Fire
http://cc.oulu.fi/~kempmp/pyro.html

Ever watch fireworks and wonder how they did that? The answer is simple: pyrotechnics. What's that? Well, find out how science and art combine at this brilliant and colorful site.

Reeko's Mad Scientist Lab
http://www.flash.net/~spartech/ReekoScience/ReekoIndex.htm

Warning: Protective goggles required to enter this site. A whole load of free and fun educational experiments on-line.

Science Daily

http://www.sciencedaily.com/index.htm

Teach your science teacher a few things with this free on-line science magazine. It will keep you in-the-know about the latest scientific discoveries and the hottest research projects around—from astrophysics to zoology.

Science/Nature for Kids - Welcome from The Mining Company

http://kidscience.miningco.com/

Make your own volcano. Sign up for a free newsletter. Many on-line activities to help you learn about your world. Plus, a gazillion links to other sites.

Sheep Brain Dissection:The Anatomy of Memory

http://www.exploratorium.edu/memory/braindissection/index.html

Not for the squeamish!!! The educational level is high but so is the gross-out factor when you dissect a sheep's brain to see how memories are formulated, accessed, and filtered by the brain. Complete with real time video!

Strange Science

http://www.turnpike.net/~mscott/index.htm

Ever wonder how we first discovered fossils? How did we even know to reassemble bones to build a dinosaur? What are some myths that people believed?

Super Bridge

http://www.pbs.org/wgbh/nova/bridge/

How would you build a freeway bridge? How about a bridge over a canyon, river, or ocean? Learn about the four major types of bridges and then test your knowledge by matching the right bridge to the right location. You might make it across, yet.

3M Collaborative Invention Unit

http://mustang.coled.umn.edu/inventing/inventing.html

An inventor looks at the world in a slightly different way than a non-inventor. How do you look at the world?

20 Things You Never Knew About Fireworks

http://www.captain-cosmic.com/f1-5.htm

Did you know that three sparklers burning together generate the same heat as a blowtorch? This and 19 other fun and interesting facts that just might make you think twice about fireworks.

The Wizards Lab

http://library.advanced.org/11924/index.html

The Wizard's Lab has experiments, a chat area, quizzes, a bulletin board, and a scientific glossary.

The World of Benjamin Franklin
http://sln.fi.edu/franklin/rotten.html

Who can claim to be a philosopher, a statesman, an inventor, a musician, a scientist, and a printer? No, not an actor with a lot of different roles to play. Benjamin Franklin was all of these things in real life. This glimpse into his life is fascinating.

You Can with Beakman and Jax
http://www.beakman.com/

Learn how to grow bacteria and gross out your friends! Learn how to make fake snot. Did you know that mucus in our noses protects us? Many more tidbits are available here.

Adventure Online
http://www.adventureonline.com/

Picture yourself an explorer? Then find out if you're up to some real challenges. Retrace Magellan's route around the world. Be the first-ever to circumnavigate the world's largest island. Go on a 1,900-mile cycling journey through Central America. Or paddle down Africa's Nile River in a kayak.

Big Top Circus Sideshow
http://www.bigtop.com/sideshow/

This is big top fun! One of the best interactive gaming sites on the Internet where you can play music on your keyboard, color pictures, watch an animated storybook, mix and match faces, and just clown around. Definitely worth the download time to play.

Biographical Dictionary

http://www.s9.com/biography/

Thomas Jefferson, Joan of Arc, and Mr. Rogers. What do these people have in common? They can all be found in this dictionary that includes over 22,000 notable people who have helped shape our world.

Boomerang Box

http://www.apl.com/boomerangbox/

Travel around the world and back again with the Boomerang Box, a large container that delivers cargo between Asia and Seattle. Visit foreign countries, hear from people in fascinating and unusual jobs, and maybe catch a glimpse of your future!

Christmas! Christmas! Christmas! from Not Just for Kids!

http://www.night.net/christmas/

It's beginning to look a lot like Christmas. Learn how Christmas is celebrated around the world with songs, festivities, stories, traditions, crafts, and activities. And best of all, there's a Christmas countdown clock to make sure you don't miss the event.

Christmas World View

http://christmas.com/html/worldview.html

Looks like Santa has his hands full. From Australia to Switzerland, find out how people around the world celebrate this famous holiday. Check out legends, traditions, and fun.

CircusWeb! Circus Present and Past

http://www.circusweb.com/circuswebFrames.html

Who doesn't love the circus? A three-ring extravaganza filled with tummy-tickling photos and rip-roaring sound.

CitySpace Project

http://cityspace.org/

Want to live in a computer? Well, this virtual city, built by kids, educators, and media artists across the Internet, comes pretty close. View an entirely navigable digital city, through stories, pictures, sounds, and 3-D models, that allows you to walk down the streets and take a look around. Even add your own street.

Cuffs For Kids

http://www.infocom.com/~hboyce/cuffkids.htm

Do you know how to be safe? Get safety tips and questions from a real police officer. Answer the questions correctly, and you'll be sentenced to fun and games.

Cuisenaire–Kid's Page

http://www.awl.com/www.cuisenaire.com/kids.html

You'll never have a boring moment again with these monthly activities, games, and puzzles. Read it, draw it, and solve it for prizes.

Social Studies

E-Conflict

http://www.emulateme.com/

Can't we all get along? Learn to bring the world closer together by knowing just how people in other countries live, work, and play.

FBI Home Page

http://www.fbi.gov/

It's the F.B.I.'s very own chock-full-of-secrets home page. See the 10 most wanted fugitives, go behind the scenes of the toughest cases, and see just how you can become an FBI agent. Click on the Kids and Teen Education Page to learn about fingerprinting, crime prevention, and how to be a Junior Special Agent!

Forensic Files

http://forensicfiles.bc.sympatico.ca/

Become an Internet supersleuth. Travel the world with Newton Beagle and help solve an international heist of an endangered species. But you better hurry before time runs out.

funschool.com

http://www.funschool.com/cgi-bin/ga?ges_usquiz,36

Do teachers come to you to ask where a state is? Prove your United States geography knowledge with this interactive quiz. How fast can you locate all 50 states? The clock is ticking.

Kids Farm

http://www.kidsfarm.com/

Life is definitely not the same down on the farm. Get the scoop straight from the animals and the people that work on real farms. But, ah, watch where you step.

Kids Window (on Japan)

http://jw.nttam.com:80/KIDS/kids_home.html

Learn about Japan while reading a storybook in English or Japanese, creating origami, and viewing pictures.

LIFE HEROES HOME PAGE

http://www.pathfinder.com/@@CAzflgcATfL9Q070/Life/heroes/index.html

Heroes exist in everyday life. Read about and view pictures of people who have made a difference in this world. And don't forget to vote for your favorite hero.

Lonely Planet–Destinations

http://www.lonelyplanet.com.au/dest/dest.htm

Your destination could be anywhere with this interactive map of the planet. Zoom in for a closer look, read information on your destination, view slides from around the world, and even send a postcard from the places you visit. All this and no lost luggage.

Mapblast! Blastoff

http://www.mapblast.com/yt.hm?FAM=mapblast&SEC=start

You are here. But where's here? You'll know soon enough as you create, customize, and print your very own maps. Just enter an address anywhere in the United States and Map Blast will create the map for you. So you'll always know where you're going—or where you've been.

NPS - Golden Gate NRA - Alcatraz

http://www.nps.gov/alcatraz/

Ready to be locked up? Take a virtual tour of Alcatraz, the maximum-security, minimum-privilege federal penitentiary that housed some of America's most notorious criminals.

Not Just for Kids: An American Thanksgiving for Kids and Families

http://www.night.net/thanksgiving/

Just why do turkeys go "gobble gobble"? All your Thanksgiving questions are answered at this truly festive site. Color pictures, read about the first Thanksgiving, cook from mouthwatering recipes, and especially, give thanks.

Pony Express

http://www.databahn.net/library/inet/history/pony/index.htm

See how the mail used to get across the United States in this guided tour. Includes a look at other former methods of communication as well.

Wall of Inspiration

http://www.auroraschool.org/WAMWEB/Introduction.htm

It started as a classroom assignment, but it had to be shared with the world. Kids from the second through fifth grades share about the people who inspire, not only them, but a world. From civil and human rights leaders to those who just made a difference.

The World's Tallest Buildings Page

http://www.dcircle.com/wtb/94.html

The world's tallest buildings have been shrunk down just for you to view. Learn how these monsters of architecture were built. Locate and check out the views for yourself.

Apollo 11

http://nssdc.gsfc.nasa.gov/planetary/lunar/apollo11.html

No, it's not some new Greek god, but the space mission that first landed on the moon. Learn about this historic event that changed a world and why it was "One small step for man, but one giant leap for mankind." Complete with pictures from space!

Ask An Astronaut

http://www.nss.org/askastro/home.html

Talk to a real live astronaut. From Buzz Aldrin to Jim Lovell, astronauts are waiting to answer your questions on space, being an astronaut, or anything else you want to know.

Space

Astronautica

http://garber.simplenet.com/

Reach for the sky and travel to the stars. If you love watching the skies, then you'll love this site. It's filled with maps of the stars and planets, guides to viewing them, and links to everything astronomical.

Astronomical Images Archive

http://www.stwing.upenn.edu/~jparker/astronomy/index.shtml

Who needs a telescope when you have access to hundreds of pictures of stars, galaxies, planets, and more, right here? With pictures being added every day, you never know what you might find in the sky.

Astronomy

http://www.educationindex.com/astro/

The stars are within your grasp. Whether you're an amateur or seasoned professional, you can find everything you want to know through more space-related links than there are stars in the sky. Well, almost.

Astronomy For Kids

http://www.frontiernet.net/~kidpower/astronomy.html

If the earth is round, why don't we fall off it? Get the answer to this and many other puzzling questions. Simple-to-understand information and full color pictures.

Basics of Space Flight

http://www.jpl.nasa.gov/basics/

Want to know just how astronauts fly through space? With pictures and illustrations, you'll learn just what it takes to be an astronaut.

Black Holes and Neutron Stars

http://www.gti.net/cmmiller/blkmain.html

By understanding the nature of black holes and neutron stars, you'll get a better understanding of how our universe works. And just what is a neutron star, anyway?

Center for Mars Exploration Home Page

http://cmex-www.arc.nasa.gov/

Is there really life on Mars? Find out for yourself when you blast off to this mysterious red planet. Experience live pictures, view charted maps, and get the latest information on our nearest neighbor.

Contact Light

http://www.retroweb.com/apollo.html

Ever dreamt of traveling to the moon in the sky? Well, the people featured here did just that. View pictures, stories, artifacts, and souvenirs from the Apollo space mission that went to the moon and back.

CyberSky Home Page
http://www.cybersky.com/

Your computer screen magically transforms into a beautiful planetarium where you can gaze at the wonders of the night sky.

Einstein's Chalkboard
http://www.sdirect.com/einstein/

Where a kid can be a kid. Filed with games, riddles, jokes, a place to get your questions answered, and a few links.

Exploring Planets in the Classroom
http://www.soest.hawaii.edu/SPACEGRANT/class_acts/

Think you have science down to a science? Then grab that lab coat and test your science knowledge with more than 25 hands-on activities that will have you exploring geology, the earth, the planets, and the infinite reaches of space.

Imaginary Planet Gallery
http://www.fi.edu/planets/gallery.html

Imagine you're a space traveler and you crash-land on a planet. How would you survive? Who would you meet? Visit your own imaginary planet to write a story of your great adventure.

Kennedy Space Center
http://www.spaceportusa.com/

The stars are within reach at this site. Blast off through the history, the present, and the future of the space program as you view actual pictures from space and even pick up a few souvenirs.

Mars Team Online
http://quest.arc.nasa.gov/mars/

Ever wanted to walk on Mars? Now you can travel right along with the probes as they search Mars for signs of life and more. Get videos, information, and photos of Mars while doing activities or talking live with NASA experts. Just watch out for Martians.

NASA K-12 Internet: LFS On-line
http://quest.arc.nasa.gov/lfs/lfsnew.html

Travel into space right on-line. The Kuiper Airborne Observatory (KAO) is a specially designed aircraft that travels above the earth's atmosphere to take better pictures of space. See how, view the pictures, and take part in the activities.

NASA Observatorium
http://observe.ivv.nasa.gov/nasa/core.shtml

Want to be an astronaut? Then blast off with NASA, the home of astronauts. Here, you can view pictures of earth, planets, stars, and other cool space stuff. Read the stories behind those images. Play games that test your space skills to see if you have what it takes.

National Space Society

http://www.nss.org/

Feeling a little spacey? This will cure you. Everything you ever wanted to know about space—including a real live astronaut to answer your questions.

The Nine Planets

http://seds.lpl.arizona.edu/nineplanets/nineplanets/nineplanets.html

Book your passage for a round-trip multimedia tour of our solar system. A must-see site for space junkies who can't get enough of the history, mythology, and scientific knowledge of our nine planets.

The Northern Lights Planetarium

http://www.uit.no/npt/homepage-npt.en.html

Take a ride through the universe, dive undersea, or stroll through the seasons at Norway's first public planetarium. Packed with the sights, sounds, and wondrous feelings of the sky above and the earth below.

SCPLS-Kids' Astronomy

http://www.co.seminole.fl.us/comsrvs/library/kids/kids_astronomy.html

Your link to the galaxy. Whatever you want to know about space you can find it here. From the planets, stars, and black holes to a conversation with a real live astronaut.

Sky and Telescope Tips
http://www.skypub.com/tips/tips.html

Learn how to view the stars and planets like the professionals. Who knows—you might just unearth another planet.

Space Race Exhibition
http://www.nasm.edu/GALLERIES/GAL114/SpaceRace/

On your mark! Get set! Go! It was the United States versus the Soviets in a race to end all races—the race to be the first in space and land on the moon. Travel back in history through words and pictures to a time when a planet's people began to dream of walking among the stars.

SpaceViews
http://www.spaceviews.com/

Watch real life views of space through telescopes so powerful you could see an ant on top of the Statue of Liberty from many miles out at sea.

Star Journey @ nationalgeographic.com
http://www.nationalgeographic.com/features/97/stars/

National Geographic now takes you on a journey through the stars. With your very own access to the Hubble telescope and star charts, you can plot your own stellar course through the cosmos.

StarChild: A learning center for young astronomers

http://guinan.gsfc.nasa.gov/docs/StarChild/StarChild.html

Are you a star child? If you love stars, then this place was made just for you. Filled with facts, trivia, pictures, and entertaining activities to test your skills—divided into levels for beginners and experts.

Stars and Constellations

http://www.astro.wisc.edu/~dolan/constellations/

You've heard about constellations, such as the Big Dipper and Orion, but did you know that they're not real? Find out all about stars in the sky, how sky watchers tell them apart, and just where you can find these non-existent constellations.

The Sun: A Multimedia Tour

http://www.astro.uva.nl/michielb/od95/

Hey, can someone turn down the heat?! Take a tour of the hottest place in the galaxy, our own sun. In these movie clips, you'll see flames on the sun larger than 10 earths. And you'll learn that the earth will eventually be scorched by the dying sun.

Virtual Trips to Black Holes and Neutron Stars

http://antwrp.gsfc.nasa.gov/htmltest/rjn_bht.html

Take a voyage through a black hole. Click on this site to see footage of what just such a journey might look like. Remember to bring a flashlight.

Welcome to Microsoft Terraserver
http://terraserver.microsoft.com

See your neighborhood from space! Amazing aerial photographs—you won't believe your eyes!

Welcome to the Planets
http://pds.jpl.nasa.gov/planets/

See the universe through NASA's eyes with this collection of planetary information and the very best photographs from NASA's spacecrafts.

Welcome to StarWeb's CyberBuzz!
http://www.flstarweb.com/teens/teen.htm

Want to navigate a spaceship? Pop some bubble wrap? Or get the latest movie reviews? You can do it all by clicking on any of these hundreds of cool links.

ALLSPORTS SPORTS CENTRAL
http://www.allsports.com/allsport.htm

Get the latest basketball score, learn how to throw that curve ball, or find out who's on this year's Bandy team. No matter what your sport, you can find great informational links here. Game on.

Sports

Ancient Olympics

http://olympics.tufts.edu/

This beautifully illustrated site takes you back in time to the days of the first Olympics.

ESPN.com

http://espnet.sportszone.com/

The place where sports fans go to die. Get the latest scores, the inside plays, and secret tips from this web site dedicated to sports. From the sports knowbies, ESPN.

Go, girl! Magazine

http://www.gogirlmag.com/

Sports, health, and nutrition for girls. Lots of articles and things to do. Always changing and never a dull click here.

A Great Physical Education Site

http://educ.ubc.ca/dept/cust/pe/

Get healthy! Learn the latest and most successful fitness techniques, read the best in education and fitness news, and cover topics relevant to teaching. Get motivated! Links galore.

The Locker Room . . . Sports For Kids!
http://members.aol.com/msdaizy/sports/locker.html

If you play or like to watch sports, then this site is for you. Learn all about your favorite sport while you practice your skills, brush up on the rules, and test your knowledge.

Sports Media
http://www.ping.be/sportsmedia/

If you're interested in sports, then you'll be interested in this site. Focusing on physical education, Sports Media brings you plans and activities to use, coaching tips, and tons of links to great sites.

Welcome to DO IT SPORTS
http://www.doitsports.com/index.html

Get to know the people behind the sports in stories, interviews, and articles. Information on cycling, running, track and field, and more.

Discovery Channel On-line
http://www.discovery.com

A little bit of history, science, nature, people, animals, and technology, all wrapped up in one place. Although not specifically designed for kids, interesting information and colorful graphic designs will keep you occupied for hours.

Disney.com – The Web Site for Families
http://www.disney.com/

The ultimate can't-stay-away-from Disney site. Mickey and your favorite Disney pals are waiting with games, activities, free postcards, electronic pets, products, events, and absolutely everything Disney! Where a kid can be a kid and more.

The Magical Music of Disney Main Menu
http://www.iaw.on.ca/~wschwart/disney/

Sing along with Mickey Mouse. Read the lyrics, listen to Midi files, or find and order your favorite movie soundtrack.

NOVA Online | Avalanche!
http://www.pbs.org/wgbh/nova/avalanche/

Go behind the scenes of a devastating avalanche with NOVA. Straight from PBS comes the series that has captured tornadoes, hurricanes, and volcanoes on film.

NOVA Online | Flood!
http://www.pbs.org/wgbh/nova/flood/

Flood your desktop with the fury of one of nature's devastating disasters—the flood. Check out the reconstruction of a flood site.

NOVA Online | Treasures of the Sunken City
http://www.pbs.org/wgbh/nova/sunken/

Map the treasures of the deep with NOVA. Dive into the depths of the sea for one of the Seven Wonders of the Ancient World: the Pharos lighthouse. Find out what high-tech tools were used to uncover and map this discovery, explore a piece of the map yourself, and learn what other treasures have been discovered.

AMNH - Expedition: Endangered!
http://www.amnh.org/Exhibition/Expedition/Endangered/index.html

Explore a world at risk in this exhibit of endangered animals. Discover why everyday animals are in danger of becoming extinct. Find out what you can do about it.

Abrams Planetarium
http://www.pa.msu.edu/abrams/

Never mind what your teachers say. Abrams Planetarium wants you to keep your head in the clouds. Here, you can reach for the stars, discover constellations, test your knowledge, and explore a galaxy of possibilities. The sky's the limit.

The Amazing Fish Cam!
http://www.netscape.com/fishcam/fishcam.html

Who's watching whom? Something very fishy is going on in this giant 350-gallon fish tank. Housing numerous colorful and exotic fish, this popular fish cam continuously displays pictures of fish swimming, right on your own computer screen.

Virtual Tours

Amazon Interactive

http://www.eduweb.com/amazon.html

Explore the geography of the Ecuadorian Amazon. Learn about rain forests and tourism. Plan your own eco-tourism project.

The Andes Expedition

http://www.nationalgeographic.com/features/97/andes/

This site takes you through the virtual autopsy of a young girl who was frozen in ice! The ice perfectly preserved her body.

Arctic Challenge

http://www.adventureonline.com/ige/index.html

Go on the first-ever circumnavigation of the world's largest island by kayak and dogsled. View live updates and breathtaking photographs. Read stories of the land, people, and animals of the Arctic. Are you up for a challenge?

The Bat Cave

http://www.torstar.com/rom/batcave/

Are bats really blind? Do they turn into vampires? Should we be afraid of them? This bat cave is open to the public and ready to drive you batty with bat facts. Explore a real bat cave, find out which bat is which, and investigate bat myths.

CAM SCAPE intro

http://www.onworld.com/CAM/

Ever dreamed of running off to faraway, exotic places? Well, now you can without moving an inch. Cam Scape displays live images from around the world.

CEU Prehistoric Museum

http://www.ceu.edu/museum/index.htm

You won't find Godzilla here, but there is a lot of information about dinosaurs. Home of the Utah Raptor, this site will get you excited about those wonderous creatures we call dinosaurs.

Collection Tours: The Metropolitan of Art [Education] for Kids

http://www.metmuseum.org/htmlfile/education/kid.html

What is art? How is it made? Who makes it? Why? All of these questions are answered in fun activities, interviews, and stories that go behind the scenes.

CreatAbiliTOYS! - The Museum of Advertising Icons

http://www.toymuseum.com/

From Tucan Sam to Mr. Bubble, CreatAbiliTOYS holds an incredible collection of over 650 advertising icons that span a century of American history. Complete with games and contests, but sorry . . . batteries not included.

Virtual Tours

The Dig Site

http://www.scriptorium.org/TheDigSite/DigSite.html

Did you know that there are archaeologists who go on digs, or excavations, throughout the world, looking for fossils, bones, and artifacts from another time? This site chronicles a dig in Egypt.

E-Patrol

http://www.sprint.com/epatrol/

Patrol and clean up the world with E-Patrol. You can learn to save energy, protect endangered animals, and make the world a better place to live. See if you have what it takes to be an E-Patrol whiz in their environmental quiz.

EGYPT FUN GUIDE

http://www.seaworld.org/egypt/egypt.html

Travel through time to the Land of the Pharaohs—Egypt. While archaeologists have studied and uncovered a world of treasures and artifacts, many questions about the lives of the ancient Egyptians are still unanswered.

Electronic Field Trip to the United Nations

http://www.pbs.org/tal/un/

From Afghanistan to Zimbabwe, the United Nations has brought a world together. Learn the history behind this powerful organization, the countries that are a part of it, and how it affects your life.

Exploratorium: ExploraNet
http://www.exploratorium.edu/

The science of hockey. A visit to Death Valley Park. Those are just some of the amazing and varied activities available at this site.

Family Explorer: Home Page
http://www.parentsplace.com/readroom/explorer/index.html

Packed full of fun activities, projects, puzzles, and more, Family Explorer offers you and your parents the chance to explore science and nature together. You don't need to know a thing about science to start and it's perfect for any age level.

Galactic Odyssey
http://library.advanced.org/11348/

Space has never felt closer. Everything you ever wanted to know about space and its exploration is housed here, under one site. Reach out and touch a galaxy, take a quick trip to the moon, or make your own predictions on the future of space travel.

Go West Sailing Adventure
http://www.gowestsf.com/

Follow the adventure of the sailing yacht *Go West* on her three-year voyage from San Francisco, California, to Key West, Florida.

GOALS: Global Online Adventure Learning Site
http://www.goals.com/

Educational adventures in Science, Technology, and Nature. Explore the Pacific. Go to the Arctic. Adventure all over the world.

Grand Canyon River Running
http://www.azstarnet.com/grandcanyonriver/

This "Unofficial Guide to the Colorado River" is officially breathtaking. Hop aboard for a river trip through the scenic Grand Canyon as you view remarkably beautiful pictures and read adventurous stories. Just don't get wet.

Internet Circumnavigation Education Expedition
http://www.circumnavigator.com/

Get ready for a 2-year adventure, around the world on a 46-foot motorboat. Answer daily nautical quizzes. The crew will be giving reports all along the way. And you can participate.

JASON VIII: Journey From the Center of the Earth
http://www.jason.org/JASON/HTML/EXPEDITIONS_JASON_8_home.html

Journey from the Center of the Earth . . . if you dare. Go to the ends of the earth on an expedition to explore the mysteries of nature. Filled with activities, information, and, of course, fun and games.

Jelly Belly Factory Tour
http://www.jellybelly.com/tour.html

A tasty treat for the mind and stomach. Go on a Jelly Belly factory tour to discover just how jelly beans are made and why you love them so much.

M&M's® FACTORY
http://www.m-ms.com/factory/fact2.html

Have all your questions answered when your favorite M&M's® take you on an amusing and witty tour that will show you just how those tasty treats are made.

McMurdo Station, Antarctica
http://astro.uchicago.edu/cara/vtour/mcmurdo/

Bundle up, because you're going to one of the coldest places on earth. Take a virtual tour of Antarctica's largest community, McMurdo Station, the central point of all of Antarctica's science activities. But, better bring along a friend because the stormy weather will isolate you from March to October. Brrrr.

Musée du Louvre
http://mistral.culture.fr/louvre/

Many of the world's greatest works of art used to be in Europe. But now, they're right on your computer! Take a virtual tour of paintings, sculptures, drawings, and more. Scroll down to the English version at the bottom of the page!

Virtual Tours

Museum of London

http://www.museum-london.org.uk/

Now you can walk the Museum of London's halls right from your own home. Find out the history of London from prehistoric times to the present day.

National Museum of the American Indian

http://www.si.edu/organiza/museums/amerind/start.htm

A history of Native Americans unfolds before your eyes in photos, art, and words. Read the stories behind the stories.

The Natural History Museum

http://www.nhm.ac.uk/

Tromp through ancient lands with the dinosaurs and swim the seven seas. With the Natural History Museum web site, discovery has never been so much fun.

Netspedition Amazon

http://hotrod.mt.ic.ac.uk/netsped/netspedition/

Welcome to the Amazon. An exotic, beautiful place where danger lurks behind every bend and adventure greets you every morning. Are you brave enough to go along on a scientific journey through this treacherous jungle?

The New York Botanical Garden

http://www.nybg.org/

A garden in the city? Believe it or not, the New York Botanical Garden houses some of the most beautiful and intricate gardens in the world. Take a picturesque tour and even talk to a gardener about the plants.

The Northwest Trek

http://www.nwtrek.org/index.html

Northwest Trek is a wildlife park. Play the game "Guess what animal I am" and other activities to help you get a feel for the park, even if you live thousands of miles away.

Parc Safari

http://parcsafari.qc.ca/english/triviae.htm

Are you as clever as a fox, as fast as a rabbit, or just plain chicken? Test your knowledge of animals to see if you're king of the jungle.

Questacon Home Page

http://sunsite.anu.edu.au/Questacon/

Explore the fascinating world of science and technology. Take a Virtual Tour, have fun with dinosaurs, enter a new dimension, try hands-on activities, experience the challenge of Puzzle Quest, and check out Comet Central.

Virtual Tours

Safari Splash

http://oberon.educ.sfu.ca/splash.htm

Great site for anyone interested in marine biology. This site includes a review of the Safari Splash of 1994 and has loads of links to more information on the Internet.

The Smithsonian Institution Home Page

http://www.si.edu/newstart.htm

America's treasure-house for learning—the Smithsonian Institute's web site is your path to a world of wonders. You'll spend all day wandering through its links.

The Sugar Bush

http://intranet.ca/~dlemire/sb_kids.html

Great rainy-day distractions. You'll spend hours reading stories of imagination, hunting down treasures, making arts and crafts, viewing pictures, and baking mouth-watering cookies or other treats from on-line recipes.

Telecom Amazon Adventure Home Page

http://vif27.icair.iac.org.nz/

Trek into the wild jungle of the Amazon River system. Meet the people and animals who live there, experience the dangerous terrain, and uncover interesting facts and information.

Terra Quest
http://www/terraquest.com

These virtual expeditions on the World Wide Web will take you climbing in the mountains of Yosemite, sailing to the Galápagos Islands, and waddling with penguins in the Antarctic. It's adventure as you've never seen it before—interactively.

Tour of Jerusalem
http://www.md.huji.ac.il/vjt/

While many travelers walk miles to pay homage to the city of Jerusalem, you can visit it in a click. Take a virtual tour with pictures and information.

The Treasured-Earth Network Experience
http://www.ten.org/

Make a wild discovery with the Treasured-Earth Network. It's your world and you can learn how to take care of it while having fun with computer wallpaper, cute and candid pictures of your favorite animals, and unpredictable, yet absolutely true, stories.

UC Museum of Paleontology Public Exhibits
http://www.ucmp.berkeley.edu/exhibit/exhibits.html

Take a trip through history to study fossils and how they link to paleontology.

UN CyberSchoolBus: Elementary Planet

http://www.un.org/Pubs/CyberSchoolBus/menuelem.htm

This interactive web site is filled with games, puzzles, and activities from across the world. Learn about the planet while challenging your friends.

The Virtual Boardwalk Tour

http://www.second-wave.com/boardwalk/

The sights and sounds of the boardwalk come alive with a tour along Atlantic City's famous boardwalk. You decide where you want to go as you relax by the seaside. Complete with historical tidbits.

Virtual Cave

http://www.goodearth.com/virtcave.html

Do you know your stalactites from your stalagmites? Browse the mineral wonders of the underground when you take a virtual journey through caves around the world. Just watch out for bats.

The Virtual Pet Cemetery

http://www.lavamind.com/pet.html

Share those special memories of your favorite friend with thousands of pet owners from all over the world. The world's largest cyber memorial holds thousands of touching epitaphs.

A Virtual Present
http://www.virtualpresents.com/

Send your favorite friend a virtual present—virtually anywhere! Pets, cars, and even tropical vacations—you can send your favorite images to anyone who has an e-mail address. All without having to cough up virtual cash.

Virtual Safari

http://www.tower.org/disease/animals.html

Take a trip through the tropics on a virtual safari. Hundreds of links to web sites where you can view live pictures of your favorite animals and obtain information on food, habitats, and anything else you could ever want to know about animals and insects.

Virtual Tour of Museums and Exhibits Index
http://www.dreamscape.com/frankvad/museums.html

An awesome site of 200 museums, exhibits and virtual trips. Most offer words and photographs, some even have sound and video clips.

A Virtual Tour of the Sun
http://www.astro.uva.nl/michielb/od95/

Make sure you bring plenty of sunblock for this virtual tour of the sun. A 20-minute journey of movies, facts, and astonishment.

Virtual Tours

WebMuseum: Bienvenue!
http://www.sunsite.unc.edu/wm/

Take a tour through Paris. Browse the galleries. Listen to classical music. This web site has assembled a beautiful collection of the world's most famous paintings.

Welcome to GlobaLearn!
http://www.globalearn.org/expeditions/brazil/index.html

A new journey in Brazil is starting. Join the team as they make new discoveries about the land and meet people. New information and stories all the time. Better than TV, any day!

Welcome to Safari West!
http://www.wco.com/~langcos/

A wildlife preserve on the Internet? Sure, it may look a little cramped but really there's 400 acres of open land where endangered wild animals from Africa roam freely. Come on a virtual safari.

Welcome to Tech Trips!
http://www.girltech.com/HTMLworksheets/TT_menu.html

Girltech has developed this part of its site for virtual trips. All for girls.

Welcome to the White House for Kids
http://www.whitehouse.gov/WH/kids/html/home.html

Socks, that presidential cat, is waiting to take you on your very own purrrrrfectly private tour of the White House. Read the history behind this monumental house and even get a chance to write your very own letter to the President, himself.

Wild Sanctuary Sound Safaris
http://www.wildsanctuary.com/safari.html

Hear the sounds of wild animals. Can you guess what type of animal is making what sound?

World Safari
http://www.supersurf.com/

Travel to Kenya, Italy, or Hawaii. This site takes you there and gives some pointers about the cultures, customs, and people along the way.

YTV: The Coolest Station in the Nation
http://www.ytv.com/

Canada's coolest and most popular kids' TV network now tunes into the Internet. Get the lowdown on all of their shows, speak your mind, and check out their great contests and activities. It's never been better to be a kid.

Dictionary of Cyberspace Slang

A new language has developed in cyberspace, but don't worry. You don't have to conjugate verbs or take a vocabulary test. It's fun to learn, easy to use, and just contains acronyms. What's an acronym, you say? Acronyms are the first letters of a group of words that are strung together, or sometimes, just a few select letters from a word. Below is a list of common acronyms that you may encounter on your journey through cyberspace.

Acronyms

2U2	to you, too	**IMPE**	in my previous/personal experience
AAMOF	as a matter of fact	**IMVHO**	in my very humble opinion
AE	in any event	**IOW**	in other words
AFAIK	as far as I know	**IRL**	in real life
AFK	away from keyboard	**KISS**	keep it simple, stupid
ASAP	as soon as possible	**LOL**	laughing out loud
BBL	be back later	**NC**	no comment
BOT	back on topic	**NRN**	no reply necessary
BRB	be right back	**ONNA**	oh no, not again!
BTW	by the way	**OOTC**	obligatory on-topic comment
BYORL	bring your own rocket launcher	**OTOH**	on the other hand
C4N	ciao for now	**PITA**	pain in the "butt"
CFD	call for discussion	**PCMCIA**	people can't memorize computer industry acronyms
CFV	call for vote		
CU	see you	**R&D**	research and development
CUL(8R)	see you later	**REHI**	hello again (re-Hi!)
EOD	end of discussion	**ROFL**	rolling on the floor laughing
EOT	end of transmission	**RO(T)FL**	rolling on the floor laughing
F2F	face to face	**RSN**	real soon now (which may be a long time coming)
FAI	frequently argued issue		
FAQ	frequently asked questions	**RTFM**	read the fine manual
FC	fingers crossed	**S & D**	search and destroy
FM	fine magic	**SBD**	silent but deadly (fart)
FOAF	friend of a friend	**SHTSI**	somebody had to say it
FUA	frequently used acronyms	**SITD**	still in the dark
FWIW	for what it's worth	**SO**	significant other
FYI	for your information	**TANSTAAFL**	there ain't no such thing as a free lunch
GAL	get a life		
GRMBL	grumble	**TBT**	talking by typing
GTG	got to go	**THX**	thanks
HAND	have a nice day	**TIA**	thanks in advance
IAC	in any case	**TIC**	tongue in cheek
IAE	in any event	**TLA**	three letter acronym (such as this)
IANAL	I am not a lawyer	**TTFN**	ta-ta for now
IC	I see	**TTYL(8R)**	talk to you later
IDGI	I don't get it	**WIIWD**	what it is we do
IMHO	in my humble opinion	**WWDWIIWD**	when we do what it is we do
IMNSHO	in my not so humble opinion	**YGWYPF**	you get what you pay for
IMO	in my opinion	**YMMV**	your mileage may vary
IMCO	in my considered opinion		

Useful Expressions

2nite	tonight	**n case**	in case
B4	before	**n/a**	not applicable
b/c	because	**to go nookleer**	to explode
cos(cuz)	because	**tripdub**	www ("triple w")
dewd	dude	**troo**	true
d00d	dude	**w/**	with
EZ	easy	**wirld**	world
grrlz	girls	**w/o**	without
guvment	government	**wuz**	was
K	1,000 (like, 2K = 2,000); also: extremely cool (k-kool, k-rad)	**wymyn**	women
kewl	cool		

▲▼▲

Glossary of Cyberspace Terms

Acronyms: A fast way of typing a phrase by using select letters from the phrase; an example is "HAND" for "Have A Nice Day"

Address: A location in cyberspace

Archie: A computer program that lets you type in a key word or words to search thousands of databases all over the world

Articles: Letters that are posted in newsgroups are referred to as articles; also referred to as "messages"

Baud: The speed at which modems transfer data

Binary: A number system that uses only 1's and 0's; this is the way computers talk to each other and transfer files

Bit: The smallest unit of information that can be sent between computers

Bookmarks: Just like a regular bookmark marks the page in a book, this marks your favorite web sites right in your browser for easy retrieval later.

Bounce: What your e-mail does when it cannot get to where you tried to send it!—"bounces" back to your computer

Browser: A program that allows you to look at web sites on the Internet

Bulletin Board Systems (BBS): Networks that your computer can dial into through your modem

Byte: A unit of information that is equal to eight bits which represents a letter (a, b, c) or a number (1, 2, 3)

Chat: Talking to someone on the computer; like talking on the telephone, only you type your words on your computer keyboard rather than talk

Command Line: The line where you tell the computer what you want it to do, by entering commands

Commercial Service Provider: A business that provides access to the Internet as well as e-mail, chat lines, and other computer services and databases

Conference: A live, scheduled discussion on-line

Cybrarian: A librarian who does on-line information research and retrieval

Cyberspace: The on-line world—this includes the Internet and the World Wide Web.

Data: Information that has been formatted so that it can be understood by a computer

Databases: Electronic file cabinets storing information in a specific category; for example, a school's database might contain information on all the students attending that school

Delurking: The moment when someone who has been in a newsgroup reading messages posts a message for the first time

Directory: The information stored on your computer is divided into sections known as directories. Each directory can contain different files.

Documents: Just like magazine articles or newspaper stories, computer documents may contain text, pictures, maps, or video clips.

Domain name: The name given to a host computer on the Internet; for example, our domain name is www.themandelkids.com

Dot: What you say instead of "period" when you are talking about Internet addresses; for example, "myname.com" would be said "my name dot com"

Download: Getting information from the Internet to your computer; once you download a file, it will be stored on your computer for retrieval whenever you want

E-mail: Electronic mail

FAQ: Frequently Asked Questions; most newsgroups and mailing lists have FAQ files which answer basic questions for newcomers

File: A "folder" on your computer, like a folder in a filing cabinet, which holds information programs, documents, pictures, etc.

▲▽▲

File Transfer Protocol (FTP): A software program that allows you to get and send files to other computers

Flaming: Unreasonably criticizing someone in cyberspace for saying something you consider wrong or just plain stupid

Flame War: When two or more people send "flames" back and forth

Forum: In on-line services, a forum is a special place for chatting about a certain subject. For example, a "home schooling" forum would be used for discussing home schooling.

Freeware: Software you can download and use without paying for it

Gateway: A computer system that acts as a translator between different types of computers to allow them to interact in cyberspace

Gigabyte: A unit of information equaling a billion bytes

Gopher: A huge directory for the Internet; it will find almost anything you're searching for

Gopherspace: Anywhere on the Internet that a Gopher program can go

Graphical Browser: A program that allows you to search for documents and sites with graphics

Graphical Sites: Places on the Internet that have pictures or links to other places, pictures, and movies

Graphics: A file containing images and pictures

Handshake: When two modems trying to connect to each other must agree on how to send data

Headers: Phrases at the start of a message that tell you what the message is about; also called "Subject Lines"

Highlighted: A word or phrase marked so that it stands out, usually by a different colored text or by underlining; in cyberspace, these are usually hyperlinks that can take you to other locations

Host: A computer that is connected directly to the Internet

Hotlist: The same as a bookmark

Hyperlink: The same as hypertext

Hypermedia: Hypertext with pictures and sounds as well as words

Hypertext: A word or phrase usually underlined and/or in a different color, that if clicked on, will take you to another location in cyberspace

HyperText Markup Language (HTML): The programming language a computer uses to create Web pages

Icon: A picture that you click on with your mouse in order to open up another page

Internet: International Network of smaller computer networks; contains the World Wide Web

Kill File: A program that allows your computer to automatically find and delete e-mail or newsgroup articles sent by someone from whom you don't want to hear

Links: Same as hypertext but can also include images, that if clicked on, will take you to another location in cyberspace

Listserv: A listserv is a program that sends and receives e-mail to a group of subscribers.

Lurking: Visiting newsgroups on the Internet without posting messages

Mailing List: Like a subscription to an on-line magazine, this lets you sign up to receive articles and e-mails automatically.

Modem: Shortcut for Modulator-Demodulator; a piece of equipment that lets your computer talk to other computers and hook into the Internet over telephone lines

MOO: A Multi-User Object Oriented environment; an interactive system accessible through Telnet by many users at the same time

MUD: Multiple User Dimensional game (also called Multi-User Dungeons); MUDs are role-playing games on the Internet that let you play with people from around the world

Net: Short for Internet

Netiquette: On-line manners; the proper way to behave while you're surfing the Internet

Network: A group of computers joined together to form one big computer by data-carrying links

Newbie: Newcomer to the Internet

Newsgroups: Sites on the Internet at which you can discuss almost any subject you can imagine; there are currently close to 17,000 active newsgroups

On-line: When your computer is connected to another machine via modem or cable, you are on-line.

Page: A document on the Internet is often referred to as a "page" or a "home page." This is what you see when you visit web sites.

Password: A word only you know that you type into the computer to open your Internet account or for access to certain web sites

Posting: Sending an e-mail message to a mailing list or a newsgroup

Postmaster: The person in charge of e-mail at a web site

Public Domain Software: Like freeware but it's not copyrighted, so you can modify it in any way you want (and also copy and distribute it for free)

Search Engines: Web sites that go onto the Internet and search for information for you

Server: A computer that provides a particular service over the Internet, such as e-mail, chat, or FTP

Service Provider: An organization that provides access to the Internet

Shareware: Software that you can download and "try out" before paying for it

Signature File: A special quote that you choose to have your computer automatically add to the end of your e-mail messages or newsgroup articles

Site: The physical location of a computer or its location in cyberspace; also known as web site

Snail Mail: Mail sent the old-fashioned way, through the postal service; slow compared to e-mail

SPAM: Sending Particularly Annoying Messages; this is done through e-mail and is the electronic equivalent of junk mail

Spoilers: Sending newsgroup or e-mail messages about TV shows or movies which the recipients may not have seen or books that they may not have read, including information that may "spoil" the story

Subject Line: A title for your e-mail message so the recipient knows what the e-mail is about

Surfing: Following links from one web site to another, like riding one wave after another when surfing on the ocean

Sysadmin: System administrator; the person who runs a web site

Sysop: System operator; someone who runs a computer system or bulletin board

Telnet: The network terminal protocol that allows you to log onto any other computer on the network anywhere in the world

Threads: Discussions within a discussion found on newsgroups or mailing lists; in a newsgroup about the environment, for example, you may want to follow a thread just about recycling

Upload: Sending information stored on your computer to another computer

URL: Universal Resource Locator; address for the location of any type of web site or Internet resource, like our site: http://www.themandelkids.com

Usenet: The collective term for newsgroups or discussion groups; there's a Usenet newsgroup for almost any topic you can imagine

User Name: The name you use to log on to the network, usually one you choose or one assigned to you by your service provider

Veronica: A search tool that allows you to quickly scan Gopherspace for directories and files

Virus: A destructive program that hides in files that you download from the Internet or receive from floppy disks

WAIS: Wide Area Information Search; another program for zeroing in on information that you're searching for

Web Browsers: Programs that navigate you through the World Wide Web

World Wide Web (WWW): The network of computers that forms the on-line world; a part of the Internet